EVOLVE

LOOK WITHIN YOURSELF FOR BUSINESS SUCCESS

PAUL DAVIS

Published by OAK TREE PRESS
19 Rutland Street, Cork, Ireland
www.oaktreepress.com

A catalogue record of this book is available from the British Library.

ISBN 978 1 78119 021 0 (Paperback)
ISBN 978 1 78119 022 7 (ePub)
ISBN 978 1 78119 023 4 (Kindle)

CONTENTS

ACKNOWLEDGEMENTS

There are so many people I have come across over the years and who, in some way or another, have contributed to the formation of this book that it would be impossible to acknowledge them all individually, but I do acknowledge and thank you.

I wish to thank my wife Dymphna for her never-ending support in my endeavours, for being my soul-mate, my confidante, my rock and my muse. I am eternally grateful to you and for the lessons you have taught me about myself.

I also wish to thank my two children, Mark and Ian, who every day make me so very proud; my parents and brothers for all the lessons you taught me, which have been the basis for the person I have become; and Frank, for getting me to see sense and putting me on my career path.

A special thanks to my brother Eugene, for the discussions we had about this book, which you were so looking forward to reading but your death came too soon and so suddenly. I thank you for the gift of being present at your passing, for teaching me one of my life lessons, and also for the strength and fortitude you have shown us all.

Thank you to Mairéad for being an angel in disguise and for introducing me to so many people who have helped me on my journey. Mary Helen, you have been a great friend and guide – thank you for unlocking me! To a really special friend, Eve, you have been a massive support – for your endless encouragement and for calling me on my stuff in a nice way, thank you. Sandra, you have been a massive influence and have given me the inspiration to reveal my gifts – thank you for your encouragement. Deirdre, you will never know how much you have helped me to heal in so many different ways. Fr. Paddy, I thank you for your insightful guidance, for reviewing the first draft of this book and for giving me the direction I needed – you were so right. To all my friends in Manresa, the Woodstock Business Conference and the Arrupe Leadership programme, I thank you so much for such wonderful discussions and challenging conversations, your input and your support.

To all my clients both past, and present, I thank you for giving me the opportunity to work with you, to be able to witness the amazing journey each of you have been on, and the successes you have achieved. To everybody who has come into my life and influenced me in some way, for the experiences you have given me and the lessons I have learnt. Thanks also to Senator Feargal Quinn, Ian Talbot, Tina Roche and Dr David Hamilton for your contributions and commentary on this book.

A sincere thanks to Brian in Oak Tree Press for believing in this book and for bringing it into reality.

And, above all, I give gratitude to God for being in my life each and every day, for being my support and guide, for helping me in my every time of need, for assisting me in writing this book and for calling me to do this work, thank you.

I also acknowledge you, the reader, for having the trust in me to take this book and to learn from it. I wish you every success in your life and in your business, and the hope that you will find your true path to making a difference in this world.

DEDICATION

To the most important person in my life – my wife Dymphna. For her support and tenacity over the years to help me get to where I am today, and for raising our two sons, Mark and Ian, to be exceptional young adults who I am so very proud of.

INTRODUCTION

First, let me tell you a bit about myself. I was born the 7th son of a 7th, which – as you are probably aware – in Ireland generally means one who possesses natural healing qualities. I have only lately come to understand that this part of me, which I turned my back on for many years, is a key element of my ability to help my business clients succeed. Writing this book, for me, is about 'lifting the veil' on who I am, integrating both my 'spiritual' and 'business' beliefs and methods, and in the process sharing what I have learned so you can 'heal' your business.

When I was growing up, I was always told there was 'something special' about me, though I never quite understood what this meant. People would come and visit me on a regular basis to have me *bless* them – a ritual I never quite understood until much later in life. When they heard what I did and the results other people were getting, they would come with all sorts of aches, pains and ailments – rheumatism, migraines, cancer, blood disorders, you name it – and they would go away delighted in the knowledge that they were *healed*. One favourite of mine was a farmer by the name of Jack, a gentle soul who was always a great laugh. At first, he came in his wheelchair, unable to work his farm, but soon afterwards he was able to get back to his farm and get rid of the wheelchair.

It was never fully explained to me when I was growing up what it meant to be the 7th son of a 7th. It was a taboo subject, as far as I could sense. I never knew what specifically I was supposed to be doing during a healing. But each time I was taken by my mother into what was universally known as the 'good room' in the house to meet somebody new, holy water was placed on my hands and I was asked to make the sign of the cross and say some prayers over the area of the body where the person was feeling pain. There was something reverent in what I was doing and everybody spoke quietly as if in a sacred place, a spiritual place. As someone was leaving, he or she would try and give my mother some money as a gift, but my mother wouldn't accept anything in return for my healing sessions.

Everywhere we went, even on holidays, it was like people just came out of the woodwork and appeared in front of me to receive a healing. I just saw it as something that I *had* to do as part of growing up in my particular environment.

The other thing about me as a child was that I loved to break things up to see how they worked. I would receive old electronic equipment from friends and relations – radios and televisions that were broken. Somehow, I was able to work out very quickly what part was broken and although I didn't know what I was doing in a technical sense, *I just knew* what needed to be fixed to make it work again. My dad was an electronic engineer in the Post & Telegraphs at the time, so I thought it must be 'in the genes'!

As a teenager, however, healing people wasn't something I really wanted to keep doing. It wasn't 'cool' and I saw it as a bit of a circus act. I still didn't know how I was doing it and getting the results I was getting. So, slowly, I began to be stubborn with my mother, as teenagers do, and I refused to meet with people for a healing. I also rebelled against formal religion as something that was rammed down my throat and that I didn't really relate to. As far as I was concerned, I had made the decision to leave all that behind me, forget about God, forget about my healings and forget about religion – sorted! Or so I thought.

Growing up and going through college and making an early career for myself, I was always referred to as being lucky. People commented that everything seemed to happen for me as if I was on a *divine path* and nothing appeared to stop me or hinder me. It was like I was always in the right place at the right time. It may sound strange, but that really annoyed me. I saw my good fortune as a result of the hard work I put into everything. If there was something I wanted, I went after it and I wouldn't stop until I got it. I was extremely focused and I still am to this day. Perhaps this is one reason I understand the business world so well.

But then I went through a patch in my life when nothing went well, my career wasn't what I wanted it to be, my personal relationship with my wife was falling apart, and I didn't talk to my birth family. I just wanted to be alone to figure out what I was supposed to do and what was wrong with me. It was such a dark space I was in, that the only option which seemed sensible at the time was to end it all.

Looking back, it was like having the Dementors from the *Harry Potter* series with me all the time, draining every element of peace, hope, love and happiness from my very being. I visited this place many times and, even to this day, I'm conscious of where it lies. But in a brief moment of desperation, with everything falling around me, I asked for help. Help from the one person I had turned my back on years earlier and that I never thought I would ever hear myself asking ever again – God. But somehow, strangely I didn't ask for my situation to be sorted. Instead, I asked for help, for me to become closer to God, to know God so that I would have somebody by my side to guide me in some way.

When I called for God's help, it was like He was there all along, by my side, waiting for me to ask, and ready to give me whatever I wanted. Like a bolt of lightning, an immediate change happened inside me. Where before I viewed God and religion with a sceptical eye, situations started to show up in my life, and as I followed them up, new and better things started to happen. I researched book after book, each one leading me onto another, all with connected themes. Slowly, I put all the pieces together, taking knowledge from different sources, making the connections and gaining true wisdom for myself. My relationships started to improve and my career took a different path altogether with the work I was doing with clients. But I still didn't know where I fitted in.

Then people seemed to appear in my life, telling me that I had an extraordinary gift and ability which I needed to develop further and use to help people and businesses. I kept dismissing them but, as I looked back and reviewed the clients I worked with in my capacity as a business consultant, I began to see trends in terms of how I interacted with them and how well their businesses performed as a result. Clients would run something past me and, somehow, I was able to give them the answers and the path they were to take in order to make it profitable and easier for them. I was able to give them the path they were supposed to take in life. It was a case that *I just knew*.

Sometimes when I talk with a client, it's as if I see the picture of where they are supposed to be and I want to guide them to that place as quickly as possible – a bit like in the movie *The Matrix*: I can *see* all the information instantly, know where they are supposed to be in life and have a sense of what is needed to be done. Also, when I look at a business, I just know exactly what needs to be fixed and where everybody fits, in the way I 'just knew' as a child how to fix those radio and television sets.

On one level, I'm a leading business development and growth specialist in Ireland, a management accountant and a certified management consultant, and I have worked with hundreds of businesses over the years through my company, Davis Business Consultants. I also have studied electronic engineering and taxation and I have a wealth of experience and knowledge to bring to clients to develop their business and to gain quantifiable results. I have all the proven tools, strategies and techniques to develop a business.

But alongside that, I have an ability to help people determine the right path for their business or their personal life, so they can achieve their true potential.

At times – even without them being aware of it – I used this ability to help clients and, when I did, their businesses would improve and new opportunities would materialise for them. Where business had been slow for months, suddenly new business began to arrive without them having to do anything. Phone calls and meetings would happen 'out of the blue' for my clients, bringing business their way, as if now finally they were on their own divine path. Top executives in large businesses would make sure they ran something past me to get my views as to whether it was the right thing for them to do, or to know what path they were supposed to take – either for themselves or for their business. As an executive mentor, I would be asked to sit in on meetings, to observe and to advise based on my own intuitive sense of what the executives should do within their business. Every loss-making business I ever worked with, I was able to turn around and their profits would increase with very little effort.

Some would say that, much like the healing work I did as a child, my work now lies in healing businesses. I eat, sleep and drink business. I'm constantly thinking about my clients and their business, and I absolutely love what I do. I love and value working with my clients and bringing them on the journey they are supposed to be on. And in recent years, I have accepted people who come to me looking for a healing. You probably could say I have found my calling.

Knowing and having my connection with God allows me to do what I do, which I am extremely grateful for. What I am is a conduit to enable healing and guidance to take place, if it is the right path for that soul to take. If you choose not to believe in a Higher Power, what I call God, *"Our Father"*, then that's OK, because you too will benefit from this book, just as my clients have done from the knowledge I share with them.

One could adopt the viewpoint that, in the business world, it's not in my best interest to tell this story. I realise that my intuitive and healing abilities will be a complete revelation to most of my clients – that my way of working is challenging and not the norm when one encounters a business executive! But as I see it, my job is to introduce the EVOLVE concept to you so that you too can discover for yourself the power that lies within us all, and begin to live a life that is more fulfilling, authentic and real. At this stage, you might still be thinking, *"What has all this to do with business and profits?"*.

Well, the truth of it is that a spiritual perspective has a great deal to do with business. I'm very passionate about business, how it works and what processes make it work more efficiently in order to return substantial profits.

I have worked across a wide-range of industry sectors, including consultancy, construction, high-tech and low-tech manufacturing, professional service, and nationwide retail. What I have found in my own research about business development is that very successful business entrepreneurs hold spirituality as a core element of themselves when doing business, albeit they also bring the other elements of striving to be the best in their field and wanting to get a good deal for the business.

I see myself as someone who works on businesses, from small business to large corporations, to improve them. I see instantly what needs to be fixed and how each person in the business should fit in (or not!) to bring the business forward. I bring the people I work with on a path to guide them to their purpose, their calling so to speak, and when they do, they blossom both personally and in their business. After clients have worked with me for a while, many of them start to develop their own spirituality, of their own volition. This then permeates throughout their business, and their business performs even better. Their spirituality affects how they interact with staff, suppliers and customers.

I also work as a confidante, personal associate and executive mentor to a lot of business owners and chief executives, for whom the highest pressure lies in living an authentic life while managing their business. The key to surviving life is to enjoy it.

My belief is that everyone has it within themselves to truly succeed in business. I mean *truly succeed*. In order to do that, however, you need to have in place some key foundations – the critical factors for success. Whether you are thinking about starting a business, are currently running a business or are a chief executive in control of a large corporation, the messages in this book are for you.

When we think of great leaders, we may think of people like Nelson Mandela, Mahatma Gandhi, Mother Teresa, or Martin Luther King. But what about leaders of our present day? Who would you look to as a good leader? Why do you consider them to be a leader? What are the qualities or behaviours of these people that help them to lead so well?

When we look at leadership, typically we associate it with power or being in charge – like being a president, a chief executive or a religious leader. But what about yourself as a leader?

You see, we tend not to look at ourselves as leaders. As an employee, you lead those around you. As a business owner, you lead your employees, your customers, your suppliers. As a corporate executive, you affect and lead your shareholders, and the stakeholders who have a vested interest in your corporation, be they your customers, your suppliers, your investors, your bankers or your community. Even as a parent, a spouse and a partner, you are a leader. In all of your dealings, you affect business. Whether you are a consumer of a product or service, or a producer of a product or service, you affect how business is done. So everything in this book is applicable to you. Whether you are a parent, a partner, a spouse, an employee, a business owner, or an executive of a large corporation, you are a business leader.

And throughout my time working with clients, I have observed certain aspects of their business leadership that make a real difference in how their business improves and how they develop as people. Being in business is the best way to find out about yourself, your failings, and what you are extremely good at. We don't fail at business, we fail ourselves. We give up, we stop at the first hurdle, or when times become too tough to handle. Is this you? Is this how you want to operate? If you were given the opportunity to change, would you?

It's not about getting to the finishing line; it's about the journey you take along the way. It's at the tough times that we need to stand back and question where we are going wrong. Success may just be around the corner and you don't even know it, because you give up just before the winning line.

In all my time working with businesses, I have found a number of core principles and laws that determine how successful we are to be – success in the stereotypical sense of the word, as opposed to my belief of what true success really is. My own journey through life has been a challenging one and yet an amazing journey. I love what I do, how I interact with people and, for me, the buzz is in seeing the difference in peoples' lives and their businesses as they progress along their own personal journey through this lifetime.

The world that we live in is an amazing place. But sometimes, we just don't stand still long enough to take it all in. We don't assess ourselves and see the part we play in everybody else's lives, and the effect we have. And even though we might do a small thing, those ripples build to massive waves right across this world we call Planet Earth. How often do you stop and stand still to look at the wonder around you? When we see the wonder in the world and how intricate everything is, and how each event and circumstance is so connected to everything, it's beyond belief how truly complex and amazing is this world we live in.

However, that is difficult to see when we are in our own dark place. We don't see anything else except the circumstances we see ourselves in, and sometimes those circumstances can be so overbearing that we wonder what is the point any more in continuing. It's the loneliest place to be in and yet it's from that space we can really appreciate what is around us every day. We cannot truly understand light without first experiencing dark. We cannot understand heat without first knowing what it's like to feel cold. This dark place has been very familiar to me over the years and there are times I felt there was never going to be a way out except for the one I made myself, good or bad.

I know what it's like to experience that place and I give gratitude everyday for what I have in my life and the amazing people I have the opportunity to be around and to work with.

So what's the purpose of this book? There are many, and so much I want to achieve for you, the reader. I want you to know that there is hope. I want you to know that there are fundamentals when it comes to building a business for the future and, if those fundamental foundations are not there, then your business will be built on only soft ground, on sand so to speak. I want you to know that you can build a business that you truly desire and that the more aligned you are to your desire and passion, then the more successful your business will be – big or small. And the more profitable it will be. I want to open you up to the possibility of doing what you love to do, each and every day of your life and still be able to make money, lots of it in fact.

If you do that, the old saying, "Do what you love to do and you'll never have to work another day in your life", will come true for you. I do that myself every day. I have a very full life. I'm extremely busy, which I'm very grateful for, and I absolutely love what I do.

It's not because I might be 'special' that I have this in my life. Everybody can do what I do; they just need to awaken it within themselves. I want to connect you with an inner source that everybody has and for you to be able to connect with that source so that you can have an extraordinary life. I want to talk about things that have had a profound effect on my life in so many ways.

When we connect with our inner selves, as everybody can, then you will be in true flow and never have to worry about anything ever again. Being in true flow means that you're in the 'zone', where you're doing exactly what you love to do, and it's as if everything in the universe is contriving to make things happen to move you forward to reach your goals. Is this what you want?

I want you to know that there is a strong reason for building a business in this way and that, if you get these foundations right, you will have a business that is sustainable for years into the future. In my own experience in working with businesses, I see that the more often these critical factors are implemented into business, the more successful the people become. My own belief is that these factors will become more relevant in doing business in the future, and businesses that don't adopt them are likely either to fail or to struggle to make a mark in their sector.

So what is contained in this book is very much relevant both for your business and for you personally. Not only that, but it's my belief that what I speak about in this book will become key aspects of doing business in the future. In that respect, as business leaders, we all have to EVOLVE in the way we do business.

EXPERIENCE WHO
YOU TRULY ARE

Values are like fingerprints. Nobody's are the same,
but you leave them all over everything you do.
Elvis Presley

Over the past number of years, the world of commerce has changed forever. This change is set to continue as more and more people come around to a new way of doing things for the better of everybody concerned, and more and more people realise the world is becoming a smaller place with communication being key. Central to this mass change in worldview are one's values.

Values might be described as 'the set of rules we follow to help us make the right decisions in life'. Some people might refer to them as 'ethics' or 'the ethos by which they live or do business'. Values are used in every-day decision-making at work and at home, and they are part of our core being.

A value is a belief, a mission or a philosophy that is meaningful. Whether we are consciously aware of them, each one of us has a core set of personal values, ranging from the commonplace, such as a belief in hard work and punctuality, to the more psychological and spiritual, such as self-reliance, concern for others, and harmony of purpose.

In business, we have to get back to core principles. Inside all of us is a GPS system of sorts. It sets the direction for us and it's what guides what we do in life – and thus our core values. Values are those inner rules that we work with, even though sometimes we are not even aware of them. They are what is important to us in life.

In the past, generally we have looked to other people for values – to the banks, politicians, and the church, even professions like doctors or accountants. We have taken on other people's values or have been told what our values are to be. We didn't take the time to choose values that we ourselves want to live by.

But, at the present moment, people are craving for our politicians, our banks, our corporations and our religious orders to have core values of honesty, openness, and honour. Observe for yourself: what are the values you are looking to see in your politicians, banks, religious orders, and corporations?

We want them to change. Why? Because we know instinctively that these are the values that society as a whole should live by.

What we inwardly believe and perceive, we project externally. It is a want that is within us, a craving.

But when did you last examine your own values? Do you know your own values? Do you live by your values each day?

You must be the change you want to see in the world.
Mahatma Gandhi

VALUES AND PROFIT

We all have values we live life by, but some of us never go through an exercise to determine what they are. Some people feel that business values should be different from personal values – why? There's no reason. In fact, the more you integrate your personal values into your business, the easier your business will become. My belief is that, first, you must determine what your core values are before you can wrap your business around these values.

You see, if your business is in conflict with your core values, then you are not being your authentic self, and your business can be in conflict with you. When you are not meeting your own values, then you are creating a dis-ease within yourself. It feels like you are not living the life you truly want to live. You are in conflict with your inner self. When you meet or work with someone whose values are at odds with your own, you may not know why there is an inner conflict with that individual, but nine times out of 10, it is down to a conflict in the values that you have *versus* what the other person has.

Do values and profit sit side-by-side? How does living by one's values in business affect bottom-line profits or return to shareholders? What happens when you're not incorporating your values into your business?

Well, let me tell you the story of the managing director of a business who I was working with a few years ago. When I was bringing my client through this values exercise, one of the values he had put down was 'fun'. When I asked him about how much fun was in his life, he answered: "Well, I can't wait until I leave my business on a Friday and have the weekend to have fun".

It was no surprise to me that his business wasn't doing as well as he had hoped, and he himself didn't have a particularly positive outlook in life.

Could fun have been incorporated into his business – absolutely, it could. All you have to think about is the environment that Google has built for its employees. Would it have made a difference to this managing director's performance in his business? Absolutely, it would. Would it have made a difference in terms of increased profits in his business? Perhaps not directly but, if he was happier in his business, meeting his values, having more fun – do you think he would have a better outlook on life, be able to see more opportunities and hence be able to improve his business, make more sales and more profits? Absolutely.

Our values play such a big role in our life and yet many of us ignore them. As I mentioned before, consumers are demanding higher values from business and values of honesty, openness, and honour will be prerequisites for doing business in the future, as will values of sustainability and concern for our community and the environment. How do your own values sit with these?

Take, for example, Nike and GAP. Because of allegations of using 'sweatshops' to manufacture their products, both businesses had to change how they went about doing business on ethical grounds because of market demands. The consumer won out at the end of the day. There have been numerous other examples over the years where businesses have collapsed as a result of the conflict of these values – not just big businesses but also small businesses.

Your own personal values are those beliefs and behaviours that are uniquely important to you, what guides your decisions in life and represents 'what you stand for'. Becoming aware of your own personal values and integrating them into your business can mean the difference between success and failure.

I work with clients to help them identify their own values. The more they incorporate their values into their business, the more they tend to realise the changes they need to make in their business.

And when these values are adopted, the more successful they are in business and in life. When their values are integrated into their business, they become more authentic when *doing* business and this is seen by the customers and clients they serve and attract.

I suggest that success and happiness come from being in harmony with your basic beliefs, because your ethics and values impact the view you have of the world. Therefore, the choices you make flow more easily. And choices and decisions are the cornerstone to success for any company or business leader.

When we examine the lives of successful people, we often see how personal values guided them, propelling them to the top of their fields – for example:

- Richard Branson – adventure, fun, competition;
- Donald Trump – winning, being tough, being the best;
- Oprah Winfrey – fun loving, helping others, honesty;
- Warren Buffett – fun, making money, fairness.

Living life according to your values is about being true to yourself. And your business needs to reflect those beliefs and encourage those behaviours, not only in yourself but in everyone who works with you. For instance, if one of your core values is to enhance and improve the lives of others, when your business reflects this belief, you are functioning and leading from the core of who you are. A business or a life that is not led by values is like a boat without a rudder … eventually, it will run aground.

WHAT ARE YOUR CORE VALUES?

To identify your core values, simply take some time out and, at the top of a blank sheet of paper, write down the question: "What is important to me in life?".

Then answer that question with whatever comes to mind, but keep going until you get at least five key words that represent your being. If you come to a blank, that's OK, just keep going until you have identified five key values. It's natural to have a mental block if you have not done this exercise before.

This is a really good way to determine your values. However, if you are having difficulty in doing this exercise, then there is a free resource that you can download directly from the website for this book (**www.thebookevolve.com**) that will bring you through a more thorough exercise in order to determine your core values.

By doing this exercise, you determine the values that are of highest importance to you. It's these values by which you subconsciously live your life and, when fhey are not being implemented and respected, you are not functioning at your greatest capacity. Engage these values in everything you do, and success and happiness will follow.

From time to time, you will come across people who have a different value system to you. This can cause unease or even conflict and, at times, you might not even understand why. Typically, it comes down to conflicting values between two persons or teams.

Let's take a typical business scenario, where one of your staff members leaves work 'on the button' at 5:00 pm, just when an important project needs to be completed for a client with a deadline that evening. You get frustrated that the client is going to be annoyed (with you!) and you are disappointed with that member of staff. However, underlying your reaction here is that you place a higher value on client responsiveness, whereas your staff member values spending time with family as more important. It's not that either person is wrong or goes about business the wrong way, it's that the two of you are different, and it's OK to be different.

But how often do business leaders sit down with their staff and explain what is important to them as owners, with all the responsibility that owning a business brings. When a new member of staff comes on board, how much time does the manager spend explaining their core values and what is truly important to them and the business. Unfortunately, most induction training time tends to be spent on procedures and processes. Many business leaders are even not aware of what their own values are and, therefore, are not in a position to express their significance until such time as a conflict situation arises.

Where there are conflicting values amongst people in an organisation, it's inevitable that things become difficult. The first thing is to identify for yourself what your core values are and then bring them into your business. People often make the mistake of building a business while ignoring their values, only to learn years later that they either don't enjoy the business they have developed or that their life is out of balance. This is one of the key aspects to making sure you build a business on firm foundations.

The core values you have identified should not be values you aspire to having. That would be like me saying I aspire to be extrovert when, in fact, I'm an introvert. We may wish we were something else but the energy it takes is far greater than just being our true selves – so I'm happy to be an introvert!

Look at it another way, if you listed 'family' or 'wealth creation' as a high value for yourself, ask yourself how much time do you spend with your family or how much money have you in investments? If the answers are not favourable to the values you wrote down, then it may be that the value you wrote down is not really one of your core values. You aspire to having it as a value but, in reality, you prioritise something else. Second, you might be like the business owner in the example I gave earlier in this chapter, where fun was a high value for him, but there was no fun in his business. You have to find ways of incorporating your values into everything that you do in life, both business and personal. Identify your values and live by them. Your life will be so much easier, authentic, and worthwhile.

The best example I have seen in my experience of working with clients who understand how important values are to business is that of a solicitor I worked with. Prior to doing the values exercise, she saw herself as a general practice solicitor. However, having done the exercise, she identified 'family' as her top value, along with 'having fun' and a few others.

While this may appear simplistic, the realisation for her was profound. She began to see correlations in the legal cases she worked on in the past that had 'family' as a core theme. And these were the cases she got the most fulfilment from. As a result of identifying her values, she then developed her practice into one that has family and child law as its main case load focus. She now has developed ancillary services to her practice, as well as a charity organisation that supports care and protection of children and young people who experience family life difficulties through family breakdown or bereavement. Her practice now intertwines around her core value of 'family'. As a result, and also down to her sheer determination and hard work, she is building a very successful practice, one which she enjoys immensely.

Determine your values and incorporate them into everything you do in life.

In this lifetime, you are a spiritual being having a human experience. For many people, it may seem that the way things are done is to separate our spiritual selves from our business, and that it's not possible to merge the two. Some believe that we should be in business to beat the competition, and that we need to be 'cut-throat' in order to move ahead in business.

But that's not what it's about. Instinctively, we want to merge our spiritual selves with our business selves. However, perhaps we don't want to upset the 'apple cart' or the norm of how things are done in business. Instinctively, we know we want our lives to be for the benefit of others. There is within us all an instinct that moves us towards a creative power, to be better, to develop and to evolve as human beings. We have a natural instinct to love and to be loved, however circumstances, beliefs, and hurts get in the way. They are our perceptions.

The perception also might be to keep spirituality and business separate. It's the way things are currently done – spirituality is something that is not talked about openly and understood in our business dealings. But is that not because it's the norm to do so? Does it need to continue as the norm? What is spirituality anyway?

Spirituality is true wisdom. And wisdom is knowledge applied. Spirituality may be defined as the spiritual practice of living out a personal act of faith, following the acceptance of faith. Spirituality can refer to an ultimate reality, an inner path enabling you to discover the essence of *who you are*, your true being, or the deepest values and meanings by which you live. Spirituality and gaining wisdom to me are very important. Where does spirituality sit with you? Have you ever considered what spirituality means for you?

BELIEVING IN A HIGHER POWER

If you believe in a Higher Power, in your own mind you may refer to this Higher Power as Higher Being, God, Universe, Source, Divine, All Knowing, Nature, Creator, Infinite Intelligence, or any other name. These are all labels, and it's not the label that is important. For me, I believe in God and that is the label I use and will continue to use where relevant throughout this book.

If you don't believe in God, or in a Higher Power, Universe or Source, that's all fine too as the principles of how you go about business and live as a person are more important.

I'm not asking you to have 'blind faith'. I want you to experience for yourself who you truly are. Have you questioned yourself on what is the meaning of life? What is your purpose? What are the questions you should be asking?

In the courts of America, on the currency, and on nearly every municipal building are written the words "In God We Trust". But do we? Do we truly believe and trust? There has been a lot of damage done over the years with abuse scandals in the Catholic Church, along with its amassing wealth, property and art. But we cannot tar everybody within the church with the same brush. There are many good people.

Whatever your view of religion is, I ask you to put it aside for the moment. In my view, religion is man-made rules, not God's rules. Much has to do with someone else's opinion or interpretation of events or scriptures or even historical events. I practice religion in my life because I have the fortunate opportunity to attend a church where the priests have 'moved on' and talk to the congregation at our level rather than the pulpit-thumping I have seen on too many an occasion in other parishes. It's a parish where spirituality manifests itself in everything that they do, and it's not even my local parish church.

I'm not telling you what is true, rather I am showing you how you can gain your own truth. In the Christian faith, we were all given one rule to live by, through the one prayer everybody was given and learnt in school: *The Lord's Prayer* – the *Our Father*. Through this, we are taught also to treat one another as we would want to be treated. So, for the moment, I ask you to put aside your thoughts of religion and to explore the possibility of something deeper and more meaningful so that you may be enabled to find your own path.

When you begin to realise 'who you really are', then you begin to realise how important values are to you and your business. If the way you show up in the world and conduct business is an extension of who you are, and values are core to who you are, then knowing what your values are puts you more in alignment with your true self, your authentic self. The more you are in alignment with your true self, the easier it is for you to make your path in life.

Now if 'who you really are' is connected with a Higher Power, then you are an extension of that Higher Power. If that Higher

Power is God, then you are connected with God always, and in all ways. If your values are in alignment with your core and with your Higher Power, then you are connected to that Higher Power, and therefore bring that Higher Power within your business.

MY EXPERIENCE

Let me put forward my experience. Perhaps there might be something to learn from it.

Imagine for a moment that you are in a space-ship orbiting Earth and that you are able to see everything that was going on – how each person was interacting with everyone else and how the minute actions and thoughts of each person were having an effect much bigger than they themselves imagined, a ripple effect of sorts. Imagine then that each person on earth was connected to each other person, as if there was an inner voice that could communicate with other people, but unfortunately the people didn't know this. They had forgotten it, so to speak, and played out their lives as if oblivious to what was really going on. They went about their daily chores, experiencing different events, pursuing their careers, interacting with other people, and searching all their life to find a feeling of true happiness, contentment, love, a purpose, and a meaning to life. They explored the world to find love and happiness and they gathered masses of wealth and materials to give them the feelings of love that they so crave. Then, one day, they reach an age when it's their time to leave. They wouldn't know anything different.

But then imagine that they did 'remember' who they truly were – that they realised that they were connected to a Source and that same Source was in everybody they interacted with. They realised what they were here for, what lessons they wanted to learn and what they wanted to experience. And that Source would guide them and look after them in everything that they did and wanted to become. All they had to do was to remember and ask.

Now, with that insight, instead of yourself observing Earth from a space-ship, imagine yourself as God and see what He sees when He looks at what we are doing on this earth. How we interact, how we go to war against each other, how we do business, how we relate to each other, how we treat each other human being, how we look after the vulnerable in our society, and the children we raise. How much love do you think is in the world? How differently do you think you would perform as a business leader with this insight?

You see, for me, God is within every one of us, and is all around us. All we have to do is remember and to connect. But I'm not just talking about having a blind faith and repeating prayers because that's what we were taught to do. I'm talking about a real connection. One that you can truly experience, understand and feel.

We can have – and be – anything we want to be in this life. We are souls with limitless power held within our small world of a body, beliefs and perception. We don't have to search around the world for love or happiness. It begins with searching within. When you realise who you truly are, everything changes. You see the world in a completely different light and you see how you play a significant role in the world for yourself, for your business and for others. You are so much more than you think you are.

God is not only in you, God is in everyone. Whatever you refer to God as – Higher Power, Universe, Source – you have the ability to connect with each human being on a completely different level when you begin to see the God in everybody. You may get a glimpse of what I mean in the simple scenes of a mother reaching out to nurture a child, a hug for a loved one who hasn't been seen for years, the caring for an elderly parent. These are natural instincts because they are more the norm.

But go deeper, and see the God within that person: the God of complete unconditional love and forgiveness. This is about connecting with people on a higher level, within our families, our community, our business and our corporations.

YOUR PART

I want to relay a story I was once told by Fr. Paddy Carberry SJ.

Imagine a picture made with mosaic tiles, a spectacular picture with hundreds of pieces, of all shapes, colours and sizes. Together, they make up the most amazing picture. As a complete picture, it's beautiful and whole. But you then notice that one of the pieces is loose. So you go over and you take that piece away.

Now imagine the picture. It's not so beautiful anymore, is it? You can see the space that has been left behind by that one missing mosaic tile. The overall picture doesn't quite look right and the colours don't seem to be as bright anymore. It's just not the same amazing picture as it was before, when all the pieces were there in their correct place. Even though it was a tiny piece that you removed, it has a dramatic effect on the beauty of the picture.

When you come to live with that understanding, you begin to understand your role in the world, where you fit in, what your purpose is and how you can connect with other human beings on a completely different level. If God is within you, and God is within everybody, then what you do to others, you are doing to God. When you approach business in this way, and how you profoundly affect the people you serve and how you are connected to each and every soul and human being, life becomes much bigger than you can imagine.

Although you may look at your life as being small, perhaps that you're not making millions in your business or fighting the cause of the vulnerable, one thing is for sure, no matter how small you feel in the world, you make a massive difference to how the world works. You have a big impact on the people you meet and interact with, even though you might not even see it at the time. Those small acts that you take for granted become tidal waves in this big amazing world of ours. Just like the missing mosaic tile, if you don't play your part in the world, it won't look as amazing as it could do.

Business is about making a profit and building assets to create more wealth. However, once you understand that your focus should not be about the money, but about the bigger picture, about the community you operate in and the difference you want to make in the world, no matter how small, and no matter what your gift or talent is, then you are building a business that will change the world. Make that your focus, make your clients a success, use the resources you have to build a bigger business that is for the benefit of all concerned, and then you are building a business on firm foundations. Never focus on the money, that will follow.

YOUR PURPOSE

Many people search the world for what their purpose is and plead to know what they are here to do. Yet all they need do is to go within themselves to find out what they need to do. They will be guided every step of the way. But, because it's not handed to us in a bright red box with a bow on top, we become too lazy to search for it, or we search in all the wrong places. And because it may not show up as being something that appears worthy of an accolade or an award, we discount it. The thing is, no matter how small you might think you feel your purpose is, it's huge in the overall scheme of things. And even though you might think that what your business does is not world-changing, it is. Everything that everybody does makes a difference, no matter how small. What is important, however, is your intent in what it is you do in life.

Again, in God we trust. However, if you truly understand who you are and you truly trust in God, then you never have to worry a day in your life. That's not to say you just kick back your shoes and everything will be taken care of. No, because again, if you truly know who you are, you would never waste a minute of any day.

One time, when I was having a conversation with a very dear friend of mine, Mary Helen, I said to her, "When I look at you, you never stop, you're always on the go, and it's like as if you *suck every ounce out of life"*. And in her very own way and with her strong South Carolina accent, she looked at me and said, "Paul, why wouldn't ya?".

I can't say it any better and any more succinctly than that. You shouldn't fear anything. Not even death.

Death should be celebrated and should be a joyful occasion. It's when the soul returns to the pure love it came from. What more wonderful experience can you get? You should fear leaving this life, not death itself. You don't want to have the ghosts of dreams unfulfilled standing around you while you're on your death-bed, longing for the experiences you didn't have and the dreams that could have been. This life is not for wasting. You need to suck every ounce out of it. Experience as much as possible, every emotion, hurt, pain, love, happiness, fun, excitement – every feeling from the feel of a gentle breeze on your arm, the sun on your face, to the ability to take a deep breath of fresh air. Your soul craves experiences. Relish each and every one of them. Stay present in the moment and take in the full experience. Don't be just a passenger on the train of life.

YOU HAVE A CHOICE

If you're sitting there and different thoughts are coming up for you as you're reading this, and your circumstances don't exactly allow the flow and ease that I'm describing, maybe it would help to remember that life is for living, enjoying and experiencing. Your business may not be performing the way you would like it, your relationships may be falling apart, or you may wish you had a relationship, you may not have the amount of money you would like in your bank account, or you may not have an idea of what you want to do with your life. But you have a choice, you can sit back and play the victim or you can release the warrior within you and realise that you have limitless power to change your own environment. Yes, stuff happens to us along the way and things don't always go according to how we might plan. But then again, we plan, and God laughs!

We have a big role to play. Yes, there are knocks and bumps along the way. Who doesn't have them? I've certainly had my fair share over the years. But that's when you pick yourself up, dust yourself off and get going, because time is moving on.

Living a life and knowing that we are all connected and that God is within us all doesn't mean you have to change completely how you do things or how you live. It doesn't mean you have to check yourself into a monastery, become all pious and walk around in sandals. That's not what it's about. It means you're able to begin to live an authentic life, a life where all your dreams come true, where you're able to build a business around what you absolutely love to do. It's where every day you wake up and can't wait to see what the day will unfold. It's where you finally remember who you are, and your eyes are truly opened. You see life in a completely different way, and the role you play in it. It's like having poor eyesight all your life up to now, and then being handed a pair of glasses that gives you 20/20 vision.

You cannot but live a life in ultimate gratitude for everything that is around you when you understand your role and fully comprehend the unconditional love that God has for you and for all of us. Can we live a life of pure unconditional love on this earth? I don't know. It's hard, but that's what we strive for. The things that are the hardest to get are the things worth striving for – but, at least, it's best to make a start.

VISION IS KEY

Deep within each one of us, there is an inner longing to live a life of greatness and contribution – to really matter, to really make a difference.
Dr. Stephen R. Covey

There are many great leaders in history: John F. Kennedy, Martin Luther King, Mother Teresa, Mahatma Gandhi and Nelson Mandela, among others. They strived to make a difference. But it all started with finding what it was they truly wanted to achieve – their vision.

YOUR VISION

Have you got a vision for your business? By this, I don't mean something that you put together on an 'away day' or have dreamed up with a marketing expert, put in a picture-frame and either hang in a prominent position in the reception area or, worse still, keep in the bottom drawer of your filing cabinet.

A vision is a statement of where you are trying to bring your business to. It's a picture of what your business will look like in time to come. This might be two years down the track or five years or 10 years. It's got to be able to paint a picture in your own mind of what you are trying to achieve.

A vision needs to reflect your own core values and what is important to you in your business – it's the main reason why you were passionate about setting up in business in the first place and the difference you wanted to make within your environment. For those of you that play golf – think of it this way: you wouldn't play golf in the dark, as you wouldn't be able to see the flag!

The purpose of having a vision is to have something definite and concrete to aim towards.

When you get into your car and your satnav asks where you want to go today, do you give it vague directions in order to point your car in a particular direction? No, your satnav needs you to punch in the exact address of where you want to go in order to guide you there. A vision acts as the satnav in your brain. The clearer you have the *address* of where you want to go with your business, the faster and more focused you will be in getting there. And I choose to believe that what you *focus* on is what you get.

WORKING TOWARDS YOUR VISION

Every day, you have actions to take towards your vision. Without having that vision, your actions are indiscriminate. Identify your vision, your desire, your dream, and then every day you can take specific actions towards what you want to achieve. Every day, you need to ask yourself, "What is the one thing I can do today that will bring me closer to my vision?".

A vision is the picture you paint for your staff and everybody who is involved in helping you achieve your dream. If they share your vision, then everybody is aligned to your focus, and the more aligned everybody is, then the more they can help you achieve it. A vision is something that you refer to as often as possible in order to make sure everybody is 'singing off the same hymn sheet', so to speak.

Some of the most powerful and influential people in the world started with a vision. The Wright Brothers started with a vision of a flying machine; Thomas Edison began with a vision of electricity; Martin Luther King started with a dream of equality for all people; and Barack Obama began with a vision of being President of the United States. Everyone who accumulates great fortunes first did a certain amount of dreaming, hoping, wishing, desiring, and planning before they acquired money.

On 25 May 1961, President John F. Kennedy gave a speech to Congress, in which he said, "I believe that this nation should commit itself to achieving the goal, before this decade is out, of landing a man on the moon and returning safely to the Earth". Most people thought this would be impossible, yet President Kennedy's vision gave birth to something much greater. By creating a vision of something that seemed impossible, Kennedy helped an entire population focus on a higher goal, which created excitement and helped to stimulate the American economy at a time when it was much needed. Kennedy's vision became a reality on 20 July 1969, when Apollo 11 Commander, Neil Armstrong, took a small step for himself and a giant leap for humanity.

On 28 August 1963, when Martin Luther King, Jr. delivered his famous "I have a dream" speech on the steps of the Lincoln Memorial, he had a very clear vision of his purpose and his goal. It had begun somewhere in his mind with a tiny speck of thought, with a notion of the possibilities that could be created with the right mindset and actions, and he took the steps and the actions to turn his vision into reality for millions of people around the world. Thus, his vision was more than local or regional, it was global.

On 20 January 2009, Barack Obama was sworn in as the 44th President of the United States. His candidacy owes much to King's vision over 40 years earlier.

A vision is the beginning of your belief in yourself, and the understanding that you can create and acquire your greatest desires and passions.

A vision is imperative for a successful endeavour because it defines your destination – where you want to go and what you want to achieve. And without it, most likely you will be caught in the tombs of what you perceive as reality, which for most of us, is usually way below the bar of what we can truly accomplish.

While a vision comes from our mind, it also engages our hearts and souls, and a power beyond ourselves that is often known as our intuition, our Higher Mind, the All-Knowing, the God within. Creating a vision challenges you to dream, and dream big, 'pushing your envelope' and encouraging you to map out and design exactly what you see for your business and your future.

Your vision is the most powerful tool you can have for your business. However, you must be careful of the vision you put together. Many times, I have seen business leaders put visions together for their businesses but it's done as an exercise, as 'work', so to speak. Having worked with clients to define their purpose and vision, I know firsthand that a vision is something that totally engages you. You will know when you have your correct vision because it will stir up an energy within you that you know you just cannot let lie.

For me, a vision is like your purpose in life, a calling. It's what you were meant to achieve in this particular lifetime. It's what you came here to do. It's an awakening and a remembering of what you wanted to achieve. Once you find it, the energy that surrounds it is outstanding and the possibilities for achieving your vision begin to materialise in so many ways, once you allow yourself to trust and believe in your vision. Then things start to happen in order to help move you forward to achieve your vision.

So many people search for what their purpose is in life. What are they supposed to do? What do they want to do? That is why the self-help industry is such a successful industry, with millions being spent each year by people trying to find their purpose. However, your purpose is lying directly under your nose. You don't have to travel anywhere to find it. You won't be able to find your purpose by reading a book – not even this one!

You find your purpose from within. Within yourself. Your purpose is your vision. It's what you are supposed to do in this life. When you go within yourself, that is when you find your true vision. By going within, you are connecting with your Higher Self and, therefore, you are able to find your true purpose, your true vision. When you find it, you will know.

The difficulty for so many people, however, is that when they find their vision, their ego takes over and comes up with all the reasons why their vision couldn't be achieved and all the reasons why they should not pursue it. They get scared because their dream is so big and then they try to bury it.

But once the giant within is awakened, it never goes back to sleep. It's then your decision whether you want to live an authentic life true to yourself or to live a life of regret.

Do you need to stand back and look at what you are doing in this lifetime? Are you in the career or business that is right for you? Do you want to live a life of regret?

Many times I carried out the same exercise to find my own true vision, and, each time, the same vision kept coming up for me. But each time, bigger and brighter. Each time, however, ego got in the way and convinced me of all the reasons why I shouldn't pursue my vision. I spoke to other people, colleagues and friends and each one of them told me I was mad, why it couldn't be achieved and who was 'I' even to think of doing something as big as that.

You see, my vision is to work with clients from around the world. Many of them are higher executives and wealthy entrepreneurs and part of the work that I do with these individuals is contained in this book, helping them on their true purpose, healing them, and helping them with their businesses. The intention is for them to truly realise 'who they truly are'. And through this work, I'm changing everybody they are in contact with. It's a ripple effect, if you will. So while I might only work with a small percentage of the population, my vision is that I'm actually affecting so many other people through the work that I do.

This book is part of the work I'm trying to achieve. It's to open people up to who they truly are and what they are capable of. Tied into my vision is a sense of adventure, freedom and fun – which are all part of my values, in which I bring all the people I work with through amazing experiences, while at the same time making a significant positive impact on the communities we work in. Given the events that have happened to me and the people I have worked with over recent years, I have seen how powerful it is to go after your true vision, your purpose and what materialises as a result.

In his book, *You'll See It When You Believe It*, Dr. Wayne Dyer makes a powerful statement when he says:

I am firmly convinced that thoughts are things. Thoughts, when properly nourished and internalised, will become a reality in the world of form. You see, we think in pictures, and these pictures become our inner reality. When we learn the how and why of this imaging process, then we are on our way to 'success unexpected in common hours'.

And, in my estimation, the most important purpose of a vision is that it stirs up powerful feelings within you that give you the motivation and impetus to move forward and create your dream, your idea, your company, your life.

Our task is not to wonder how we are to achieve our vision, our task is to remember and focus on that vision. Throughout your life, if you listen to your Higher Consciousness, and observe what is around you, you literally will be shown the path to obtain your vision.

Some people, however, get impatient and want to achieve their vision as quickly as possible. They want to know each and every step along the way to achieving their vision. True mastery lies in allowing yourself to be in the present moment. When driving your car at night, you can only see the road a short distance ahead. You know where your final destination is, but all you need to see is the short distance in front of you.

LISTEN TO YOUR INNER SELF

When figuring out what you can do for your business and how to evolve and innovate, be silent and start to listen to your inner self, your Higher Self, your soul's voice. Maintain your focus on your vision and each step to your vision will be presented to you in the most remarkable ways.

My belief is that we all are born with a plan of what we should do in life. The problem is we forget what that plan is. As a child without limitations, we dream and start to take actions towards that plan. But as we get older, we get distracted and we find it harder to remember what our purpose is. Events get in the way and take us off track. We have an unease in what we are doing. Part of our purpose is to remember and then take action towards that higher purpose. By spending time developing your vision, you are tapping into an energy that is boundless, and everything is brought into being to help you achieve your dream, your purpose.

Part of the work I do with clients is being able to see the picture of where they are supposed to be, what they are to do and their purpose. Sometimes, I get amazing pictures that it's nearly impossible to describe to my client. It's like we are all on a train track going through life. However, for most, only one side of the engines wheels is on the track, and the other side is riding along the gravel at the edge of the track. We are going somewhat in the right direction, but it's not easy. At times, we may feel like giving up and doing something else. Part of my work is seeing that picture for clients, and then putting all the wheels of the train engine firmly on the track. Once this is done and I engage with clients, amazing things begin to happen and opportunities start to show up for them which get them closer to their dream. Countless times, the results have been astonishing.

They are in a state of flow and focused. Being in a state of flow is where everything seems to happen automatically, coincidences start to happen, meetings and people we need to be in contact with to help us move forward begin to appear as if by chance. Everything that you need just shows up unexpectedly. You're doing exactly what you are supposed to be doing and loving every minute of it, and it doesn't drain your energy. You could be in your flow but not even aware of it. Things 'just happen' and you don't even realise it.

At this moment for you, do you feel everything is working well for you? Do you feel you are in this sense of flow? What meetings, events or people have showed up for you recently that you weren't expecting but ended up helping you with what you're trying to achieve?

One of the comments that's regularly said about me by clients is "Just do what Paul says and you'll get places". Just like when I knew exactly what had to be done to fix the radios and televisions as a kid, when I'm working with a business leader, I just know what exactly needs to be done for them and their business in order to make it work. I've had situations with clients where, before working with them, their business had been a significant struggle. Once I get them onto the right track, their turnover increases, new clients come their way, they get media exposure that helps them get their name out there without them having to do much, and the opportunities they get presented with are amazing.

However, others take their time to follow the advice I give. I had a client recently who had me work with them for a year. On our very first consultation together, I told her exactly what she needed to do with her business. She struggled and fought with me and yet her business wasn't working. She finally agreed to make the decision to completely change her business in line with my suggestions and, within a month of making that decision and following through on the plans, she obtained media exposure and the doors were opened for her with access to sufficient clients that she could retire on. That's how important it is to make sure your vision is exactly what you are supposed to be doing in this lifetime, no matter where you are in business right now.

GETTING BACK ON TRACK

There are times, however, that the train that my client is on – their vision – has gone so far off track that the direction they are going in is too far off where they are supposed to be. When I describe the picture to them of where they have to get to, it's so difficult for them to see it for themselves or it appears too difficult for them to achieve, that many of them decide to continue going on the path that they are used to, no matter how uncomfortable or difficult it is for them. These cases are heartbreaking, but only they have control over their will.

Recently, I came across a designer who, even though she somewhat enjoyed the work she was doing, her business wasn't doing very well. I described the kind of design work she should really be doing although it would have meant designing in a different industry. I knew in my heart that she would be extremely successful at it but, for her, it appeared too difficult to achieve even though she agreed it was where her true passion lay. So she decided not to pursue it. That, for me, is when it's difficult not to get too attached to the outcome but I know that, at some point later on in her life, it will more than likely reappear. If you don't fix something now, it is more than likely going to reappear as a choice point until such time as you do decide to pursue it.

A choice point is a time in your life when everything may appear to be falling apart for you: your family, your business, your finances, your health, your relationships. There are different routes you can choose to take along your life path: each one of them within your control, and each one of them giving you different experiences and lessons. You can ignore these choice points and continue to go along the same path you've always been on or you can choose a different path, a different course in your life. It's always your choice.

Deep down within you is a desire and a passion to achieve something, whatever that might be for you. Your Higher Mind knows what that is. It's your key task to tap into that desire and make it a reality.

Once you have awakened your vision, it's then important to keep that vision alive. The importance and purpose of visualising is not a new thought form, it has been around for centuries and used by people who are now names in our history books. First published in 1912, *The Master Key System*, written by Charles F. Haanel, declared:

Visualisation is the process of making mental images, and the image is the mould or model which will serve as a pattern from which your future will emerge.

Exercise caution though. Partly as a result of many popular self-help and business strategy books, a lot of people believe that, if they simply visualise a picture of what they want, it will appear out of thin air. There is nothing more wrong than this. To my mind, these popular books did some good, but equally they did a disservice. Primarily, these books raised an awareness around the world of something much greater than ourselves and something that has been around since time began. And this awareness has been amazing.

However, what these books fell short of is something else entirely. Visualisation is not simply putting an image into your mind of what you want to create, although there are countless people making money selling this belief. It's also about taking action. Visualising, in my mind, is another word for connecting with your inner soul, your Higher Consciousness, your God. Your Higher Self has all the answers for you and what your soul truly wants.

WORKING WITH YOUR BELIEF SYSTEM

Earlier in this book, I wrote about my connection with God. In my mind, it makes no difference what name you decide to put on your Higher Mind, Higher Self, Higher Consciousness. It's what works for you and your belief system. For me, it's easier to see my Higher Mind as God and this is what I truly believe.

The main thing is that, once you connect with your Higher Mind, you are connecting with your true self, the unconditional part of you that loves you more than you can even imagine and wants to give you more than you can even think possible. You will know when you have connected with your Higher Mind. The passion, the desire, the boundless emotions that well up inside of you are your indications to you.

In her autobiography, Saint Teresa of Avila describes the most exquisite beauty of this inner knowing. Where the popular books I referred to earlier fell short was in a failure to make that connection for the reader so they could comprehend what true visualisation really means. It's you connecting with the God within you. As Marianne Williamson says:

> *It's not just in some of us, it's in everyone.*

TAPPING INTO YOUR DREAMS AND DESIRES

We all have dreams, ideas, thoughts, purpose, passion – but many of us don't tap into them as we move forward with our lives. Creating your vision gives you the opportunity to tap into your passion and inner longing, and connect it with your dreams and desires.

Your vision begins with your desire for what you want to create, what you want to achieve, and the difference you want to make. A vision can be small or large, as long as it's based on your true desire. Instead of just having a thought about your business and the kind you want to create, starting with a vision encourages you to go deeper, dream bigger, connect your thought to pictures in your mind, engage your passion, identify your purpose, and open up the opportunities and possibilities that will help you bring your idea into reality.

> **But a word of caution: it's not just about the money. When you make money the primary focus, then nothing will work for you, especially in business. Now this may seem strange coming from an accountant, but it's true. Yes, financial reporting is important. But don't make money your primary**

focus in life and in business. By doing so, you are giving it a higher power than yourself.

The most successful people in business don't have money as their primary focus or motivation. Yes, they value money, but it's not their focus. Their focus is being the best they can be in their industry.

Look at Warren Buffett, Richard Branson, Oprah Winfrey or any other person you see as being successful. When they initially started out in business, it was keeping their focus on their vision that made them successful; their focus was not on the money. They are competitive and constantly strive to be the best. They have a strong vision of where they want to get to and their passion is engaged. When these elements are brought together, anything is possible. The money then flows. It's as if it's a resulting bonus, but it's not the main focus.

Dr. Stephen R. Covey, author of *The 7 Habits of Highly Effective People*, states it nicely: "Start with the end in mind". This relates to everything you do in life and in business. Start with where you want to bring your business to. What is your dream, what is your desire? What do you want to achieve and what difference do you want to make? We all have a much bigger game to play in life, so why limit your possibilities?

But, more importantly, your vision has to be a "burning desire" as Napoleon Hill puts it. It must be something that you truly want to achieve, something that you 'lust' after, if you will. Something that you think about night and day and that stirs up the true essence of you.

When you truly connect with your Higher Consciousness, the emotions inside of you will be intense and the dream of what you want to create will drive your passion. It's with this passion that you truly begin to accomplish what you want. It drives you and becomes you. It's your 'burning desire'. When you realise who you truly are, you engage with life on a completely new level and what you can achieve is amazing.

OPEN UP TO YOUR PURPOSE

We were born to make manifest the glory of God that is within us. It's not just in some of us, it's in everyone.
Marianne Williamson

As in building anything, there are steps to creating a vision and questions that need to be answered to help you begin building the 'picture in your mind' of the successful business and life that you intend to develop. An essential part of building a vision is engaging your intuition – that part of you that has wisdom, depth, and foresight beyond the capabilities of your mind.

Through the practice of meditation, you can begin to connect with your Higher Self. Come to your Higher Consciousness in silence.

Here are some steps you can take to get you started.

STEP I: ASK YOURSELF: "WHAT DO I REALLY WANT TO BE DOING?"

We all have passions – things that we enjoy doing so much that when we are engaged in them, time seems to stop. What are your passions?

Every successful entrepreneur has passion behind what they do. They believe in their service, their product, their mission. A piece of themselves goes into every part of their business.

So identify your passion. Perhaps you know exactly what it is and you can begin building your vision of engaging your passion in your existing business or in your future endeavour. But for many of us, this thought process and approach is totally new and different, and we don't have the slightest idea of what our passion may be or how we could create a business around it. If that is the case for you, it's important that you engage your intuition, the innate wisdom that resides within you.

The first step to begin your 'vision quest' is to take some time to be by yourself and get quiet. Then begin by taking deep breaths to settle your body and your mind. As your body and mind settle into a quiet place, begin to ask yourself these questions:

- What am I passionate about?
- What kind of business or endeavour do I want to create?

- Along with my passions, do I have a purpose that I would love to achieve in my lifetime?

Continue to breathe deeply as these questions form in your mind, and then release them out into space, letting your thoughts float through the possibilities and dreams that might be hidden in the far corners of your mind. Don't censor them. Don't try to label them or put them 'in a box', simply let them come.

And go beyond today into the future and imagine your life in two, three, five, eight, or 10 years from now. What do you see? Visualise your business. What does it look like, feel like, sound like and even smell like? What size is it? How many people work with you? What products or services do you offer?

As your questions float through your mind, a picture will begin to form and new thoughts will appear.

STEP 2: WRITE DOWN WHATEVER COMES TO MIND

Don't assume that you will remember these thoughts, ideas, and pictures once you step back into your daily routine. Write them down. Capture them on paper. Help them start to become a part of your reality by putting them into written words.

Don't judge yourself in this process. Write down everything and anything that comes into your mind. Don't question it; don't judge it. This is the part of the process where you are open to all possibilities. Even if the thoughts or pictures in your mind seem unachievable or outside of your realm ... don't think, just envision and write it all down.

It doesn't matter if it feels impossible or unattainable, write it down. When the vision of a man walking on the moon was first thought of, it seemed impossible, unimaginable, unattainable ... yet at this point in history, several people have walked on the moon and it no longer is impossible or unimaginable. You have to dream it to achieve it. Remember Robert G. Allen's comment:

The future you see is the future you get.

STEP 3: DON'T IMPOSE LIMITS ON YOURSELF

It's our human tendency to want to impose limits or tell ourselves what we cannot do. Don't let yourself do that. Let your ideas continue to flow as you write down your passions, your possibilities, and your dreams. When Henry Ford had the vision of creating a motorised vehicle for ordinary people, everyone thought he was crazy, that it could never be done. But he continued to believe in his vision and his ability to make it a reality. And his ideas and his vision are still impacting people's lives today.

Walt Disney had a passion and a vision that took a simple drawing of a character and turned it into a business dynasty that even today, over 40 years after his death, millions of people all over the world continue to enjoy. With the power of his ideas and visions behind him, Disney turned his drawing of a mouse into a talking, moving character that is still well-known 80 years later.

STEP 4: DREAM BIG

When you've got to the point that you don't have any more ideas, push your limits and your dreams even farther – dream big, dream huge, dream the impossible. You are now in the creative process of designing your vision. Don't let fears, doubts or lack of faith – in yourself, a Higher Power, or the universe – stop you from dreaming as big as you can. Write it all down. As Donald Trump says:

If you're going to think at all, think BIG.

Have a dream bigger than yourself. When you are looking at your vision, does it excite you? Does it inspire you to move forward? Does it motivate you? If not, you must allow yourself to dream bigger. Your dream is what gets you up in the morning. Your dream is the purpose of your very living. You have a mission to complete and nothing should stand in your way. You may not be able to see your complete plan yet in how you're going to achieve your vision, but you will achieve it.

Do you have what you believe to be an impossible dream of owning a big company? Don't stifle the dream. Put it on paper. When you think you are finished, ask yourself how could it be bigger? Keep going bigger and bigger. You will know when you have arrived at the right vision for you because the feeling inside of you will be much different, much more exciting, and a part of you will know deep down that it's actually possible.

Cherish your visions and your dreams as they are the children of your soul, the blueprints of your ultimate achievements.
Napoleon Hill

STEP 5: IF YOU HAD UNLIMITED RESOURCES, WHAT WOULD YOU DO?

Now stretch your list even farther by thinking about what you would be doing if money were no concern. Where would you be living? What activities would fill your days? What would your life look like?

Write it all down, adding to the list of dreams, passions, possibilities, and purpose you already have.

Again, Napoleon Hill advised:

Remember, no more effort is required to aim high in life, to demand abundance and prosperity, than is required to accept misery and poverty.

STEP 6: WHAT MAKES YOU HAPPY?

After you have written down every passion, dream, and possibility, take a moment and just relax. Enjoy the process of creating your dream, your vision, and your life. And then look at your list. Read each entry and highlight the ones that bring a smile to your face and a feeling of happiness to your heart. Those are your beginnings, your possibilities, the small specks of thought with which you can begin to build a business that is centred around your passions and your dreams.

Don't skip this step because designing your business and your life around what makes you happy is an important piece to the overall puzzle of building a successful enterprise.

STEP 7: SUMMARISE THE PICTURE YOU HAVE JUST CREATED INTO A SENTENCE

Now take your small specks of thought and possibilities and create a statement of your vision: your goal. Put some time into this part of the process. During the beginning steps of this undertaking, you have engaged your subconscious mind, which as Napoleon Hill so aptly points out in his book, *Think & Grow Rich*:

> ... *draws upon the forces of Infinite Intelligence for the power with which it voluntarily transmutes one's desires into their physical equivalent.*

So use the information that you have just gained from your subconscious to consciously create a statement of what you plan to develop, create and build. This statement will be the beginning step for bringing thoughts into actions and methods – for taking an idea and creating a reality.

> *Whatever the mind of man can conceive and believe, it can achieve.*
> Napoleon Hill

STEP 8: NOW DEFINE A BUSINESS THAT CAN ENCOMPASS YOUR VISION

Your vision is now your starting point. Let's say that your vision is to create a company that makes delicious and healthy baked goods, using only the best ingredients. Expand on that vision. Begin by envisioning the products, the building where you will make them, the tools you will use.

Begin to ask yourself questions that will help you start to define your business. Where will it be located? Will it begin as a home business and expand? Will you buy or lease a building? What will you do differently from the companies currently in the industry? How will your business reflect your purpose, your values, focus, and direction? Where will the finances come from to create your business? (And don't let this question stymie you – successful entrepreneurs all over the world and throughout history have begun with little or no money and, with intuition and ingenuity, have found the resources they needed to accomplish their goals).

Let the questions continue and the details flow to take your vision statement into a drawing or a plan. You are now completing the details of your destination so that your innate navigation system can help you create the roadmap to get you there. Be complete and precise. This step will make the difference that can be compared to telling your car's satnav where you want to go, the specific street, address, and building. The more detailed you are in your description of your destination, the more easily your Higher Power can help you get there.

So, question, think, and design. Again, don't censor or put limits on yourself. Imagine the building as big as you have a desire to imagine it … but, if your desire is to start with a small building, don't criticise your desire. Let your desire and vision develop as your intuition guides. Your vision may, and most probably will, change as your business becomes a reality and opportunities open for you. As you begin your journey, understand that the vision you have now may be a bit different tomorrow, and quite a bit different a year or two from now … but that's OK. In fact, it's an amazing part of the whole process of having a dream, an idea, a vision.

So plant the concept in your mind that, as you achieve your initial vision, you stretch yourself again. Be willing to constantly step outside of the box as new ideas come, opportunities present themselves, and success begets more success. Being a true entrepreneur means constantly striving to be the best in your field and evolving as the environment changes.

At times, visions can be so grand that they seem impossible, and many people around you will doubt you, your dreams, and sometimes even your sanity. They did for me! But it's your life, your dream, and your vision; the only person who really needs to believe in it is you.

STEP 9: GET SPECIFIC IN DEFINING WHAT IT LOOKS LIKE

This step is similar to building the rooms inside a house. Once you have decided where your home will be, how large it will be, and what it will look like on the outside, the next step is to start marking off space for the rooms, their size, and their location within the home. So narrow down the details of your business even more.

What day will you open the doors of your new business? Will you be selling to consumers or other businesses? What will the mission of your business be? As a board of directors, what is it you want to achieve? What kind of a business leader do you want to be? What kind of business atmosphere do you want to create? What is your intention around building your business?

As you answer your own questions and build the details around your business, stay focused on the intention of your end goal, your purpose. Donald Trump said it so succinctly:

What matters is where you want to go. Focus in the right direction!

STEP 10: GIVE AS MUCH DETAIL AS POSSIBLE

Ask yourself the question – what does your business look like when it's finished? If you were building a house, this step would be where you would decorate the interior of your home ... where you paint the walls, add the carpet, buy the furniture. Do the same thing as you envision your business.

And don't get stuck on worrying that 'it has never been done before'. In 1975, Bill Gates started with a vision of a computer on every desk and in every home – at a time when you couldn't even buy a personal computer.

Using the example of building a business that creates healthy baked goods, smell the baked goods, see them, taste them in your mind's eye. See the people who will be helping you create your product. Imagine the consumers who will be buying and enjoying the delicious and healthy baked goods that your company will be making. Envision every detail both small and large.

As you supply the details, have trust in your Higher Mind, in a power much greater than you, that every small detail that you imagine can happen. You don't have to know how this is going to be achieved at this moment in time. Once you have created your vision and focus, ideas, possibilities, and opportunities will open for you. 'How' is not important right now ... just know that they will. Trust Walter Russell:

> *Down deep in his heart, he knew that we all have the same promise of the unlimited help of the Universal Intelligence that guides all things. If we want it, we only have to plug into it with the master keys of desire and trust.*

Knowing your vision for your business is a powerful tool for achieving your goals and creating a successful venture. Your vision is an instruction to your mind so that it can help you design and implement the steps and processes that will be needed to bring your ideas into a fully-functioning, successful endeavour.

You will achieve a focus and clarity about what it is you want to do, enabling you to work out a path of how to get to where you want to go. It will mean creating a business that is based on your core values and reflects the real you, where your true passion and desire infuses your business, where you are doing exactly what you love to do. Surround yourself with people who will assist you in achieving your dream and feel a sense of purpose. With your vision, it will enable you to be more strategic with your business as opposed to being tactical and dealing with just the day-to-day issues. More importantly, you will know when you have arrived at your destination.

Sometimes, we can take the long route to our destination, other times we can take the motorway. No matter which way you go, if you're determined and focused on your vision, you will get there.

There are times when we need help along the way. Every successful person has a mentor, a guide, a personal associate to keep them on the right path. It's how my clients move so fast.

At times along our journey, however, we have lessons to learn and choices to make. And how you make those choices determines what route you take – the fast route or the slow route. At some choice points, you might consider 'checking out' altogether or you might see them for what they are, blast through them and move on. Other times, you might just give up on life and resign yourself and your circumstances to being at the mercy of others or the environment. However, it's at these times you need most to take responsibility for your life. These choice points are to lead you to your purpose, your life lessons and, ultimately, to a much more fulfilling life.

Once you know where you want to go in business – what your vision is – the next step is to recognise exactly where you are at the moment and to develop a path to get from where you are, to where to want to be. By looking at where you are and clearly defining where you want to get to, the process becomes similar to joining the dots. You will be able to map out clearly the steps you need to take to bring your vision from a concept to a profitable business.

As you develop your vision, you begin to fill in details of where it will be, what it will look like, what your products or services will be, etc. In this way, you begin to use the pieces that you define to put together the entire puzzle. Planning and strategising is essential for the success of any business. As the maxim goes:

No one plans to fail; many just fail to plan.

OUR GIFTS AND TALENTS

If you enjoy what you do, you'll never work another day in your life.
Confucius

Many of us go through life doing something that we think we like, but deep down inside, we know there is something else. We stay in our current field because it's what we are trained to do.

We all have natural talents – things that we are innately good at and enjoy doing – which we may not be using in our current careers. It's what happened to me when I turned my back on my own gifts and my connection with God. Some of us may not even realise what our natural talents are, and others take these abilities for granted without recognising their potential for changing their lives and other people's lives. Combining your natural talents with your passion is the next step to being a successful business leader.

When I was developing my own career, I trained as a management accountant. I'm really good at it, and from wanting to help my clients more, I later studied taxation as I began to get more and more involved in buying and selling businesses.

However, learning to be an accountant is learning a skill. We can learn it and perfect it, but at the end of the day, it's still something that we have to work at – it draws our energy. A talent, however, is something that comes naturally to us. We do it without even thinking – it draws no energy from us. It wasn't until 2004 that I realised for myself the importance of this. Only then did I realise that it wasn't the accounting work that I loved, but that I was fascinated by how the accountancy and taxation worked together and their effects in a business, which is very different from what you would typically do as an accountant.

I then decided not to take on any more 'accounting' clients and started to engage with clients on a completely different level, one that was in sync with my own innate talents. I started to guide them to what they should be doing and how they should develop their business. As a result of doing so, my work is easier and much more enjoyable. I absolutely love what I do. I now use my accounting skill to monitor the performance of my clients' businesses and to interpret the results as opposed to doing the accounting work as a primary focus.

It's the difference between constantly having to work at something to improve your performance in it as opposed to doing something that is natural to you, and you truly love to do. Take a pianist, for example – you can learn and train to play the piano, and practice it every day so that technically you can play a masterpiece. And many people over the centuries have done this. However, you also can encounter a pianist who can play the piano naturally. Yet when he or she plays, while everything is technically correct, he or she also is able to connect with the audience on a completely different level, a soul level. The experience from the audience's perspective is completely different between both pianists. ·One hears from time to time an audience member reacting to a virtuoso performance with "She is gifted". This is the difference between somebody who is truly using their innate gifts or talents as opposed to somebody who is simply working well with their skills.

My belief is that we all have a purpose in life and we all have innate gifts and talents that, when recognised and integrated into our business and personal lives, help us to achieve a level of success that we couldn't achieve without using those talents. Some good examples of people who have recognised their talents or natural abilities and have built careers and amazing lives with those abilities are:

- Michael Flatley – Irish dancing.

- U2 – pop music.
- Michael Jordan – playing basketball.
- Tiger Woods – playing golf.
- Oprah Winfrey – influencing and inspiring people.
- Dr. Seuss – a keen sense for nonsense.
- Mother Teresa – compassion and empathy.
- Donald Trump – business sense.
- Jim Henson – making puppets come to life.

Some of you know exactly what your gifts and talents are, and incorporating them into your vision and your business is already a part of your plan. However, for others, you are aware of your gifts and talents, but you have never believed that you could make a living using them. I hope from this book you understand that you can create the opportunity to do just that.

Like me, oftentimes, we don't recognise our natural abilities because they are a part of who we are and we don't see them as being anything special or particularly useful or we think other people can do what we can do. By taking on board what's contained in this book, you will have pinpointed what you like to do, and have a vision about what you want to do. The next step is to identify what natural talents will play into that passion.

It's actually quite simple – if you have a passion for something, you have an innate gift or talent that supports and compliments your passion. You might not yet have honed those capabilities, but they exist under the surface of what you love to do. Your gifts and talents are like unearthed treasures waiting for you to discover them. Identifying and embracing your talents is much like carving a statue from stone or digging for buried treasure, you keep carving or digging until something magnificent appears – in Michelangelo's words:

I saw the angel in the marble and carved until I set him free.

Natural talents are often things we use daily and don't give any thought to such as:

- Being organised.
- Knowing how to make plants grow.
- Having the ability to cook delicious meals from recipes.
- Easily developing a connection and rapport with people.
- Being a good listener.
- Having an ability to communicate well.
- Being good at all things mathematical.
- Being a good conversationalist.
- Having an ability to write well.
- Having a great sense of humour and ability to laugh at yourself and not take life too seriously.
- Easily relating to people.
- Having a natural ability for sales.
- Being able to talk with almost anyone about almost anything.
- Having a great creative imagination.
- Being a very caring, nurturing person.
- Having artistic abilities in the fields of acting, writing, singing, or playing an instrument.
- Being very perceptive.
- Having a natural ability to explain or teach.
- Having a great analytical mind.
- Being able to inspire and motivate people.
- The ability to develop trust quickly.

There is a variety of gifts but always the same Spirit; there are all sorts of service to be done, but always to the same Lord; working in all sorts of different ways in different people, it's the same God who

> *is working in all of them. The particular way in which the Spirit's*
> *given to each person is for a good purpose.*
> St. Paul, *Corinthians*, 12:4-4.

If you cannot identify your natural talents quickly, start to listen to what people say about you. Ask people who know and love you what they believe your natural talents are. Look at areas in your life where you have excelled – what abilities helped you to do so? When you were a child, were you consistently told that you were very good at something? If so, what was it? When you lose all sense of time, what are you doing? What comes very easy to you while others struggle to do the same thing? Is there something that you do much better than anybody else you know?

When it comes to work and career-related abilities, the following questions can trigger your thought process:

- Do you currently enjoy what you do?
- What do you love to do?
- What comes naturally for you?
- What gives you fun?
- What situations in the past did you really enjoy? Why?
- Is there a trend showing up in the type of work you love to do?

Just asking yourself these questions might help you identify and pinpoint your natural abilities and talents. If so, make note of them and put them with the worksheets you used to create your vision.

If you still are unable to identify particular talents or skills, the process for discovering your natural talents is very similar to the one used to unearth your vision. It involves giving yourself the time and space to let your thoughts and ideas make their way into your conscious mind. In a quiet place, take some time out by yourself and start to list 20 talents that you believe you have. No matter how long it takes, stick with the exercise. More than likely, you will hit a point when you have put a few talents down on paper and then you hit a blank and can't come up with any more. But make sure you keep at it and wait for them to come to you. Begin to remember what positive things people – teachers, family, friends, clients and colleagues – have said about you over the years, about what you do and how you work. List them all down. Don't pressurise yourself, just take your time and keep with it until you have your list of 20 talents. Then you can go back over the list and identify those talents that you can see are closely linked to carrying out your vision.

In his book, *Authentic Happiness,* Dr. Martin Seligman writes about the importance of knowing and incorporating our "Highest Personal Strengths" into our life and everything we do. Dr. Seligman has identified 24 strengths, from curiosity and love of learning to humility and humour. The book teaches us how to use these strengths to create a happy and powerful life. And he believes that each one of us has "Signature Strengths," that a person:

> *... self-consciously owns, celebrates and (if he or she can arrange life successfully) exercises every day in work, love, play and parenting.*

On his website, **www.authentichappiness.org,** Dr. Seligman offers a VIA Strengths Survey that can be taken to help you identify your strengths from top to bottom and then compares your answers to thousands of other people. Dr. Seligman says:

> *Knowing your Highest Personal Strengths can help you consciously include them in the process of creating and running your business.*

When you create a business or a corporate position around your natural talents and personal strengths, not only will you enjoy what you are doing, it will be easy to excel because of the passion you have for your business and the innate abilities that you bring into it. You are there for a reason – even if that reason is not obvious to you. You need to identify your own gifts and talents and how they can be incorporated into the business. You need to determine where your passion lies and where you would like to take the business along with your executive team. Combining passion and abilities creates an environment that people will gravitate toward.

Look at the Starbucks coffee chain. There are other coffee companies in the world and certainly other coffee houses, but the passion that the people behind Starbucks have for their product and what they do is evident in every facet of their business – their products, their coffee shops, their marketing, their packaging, their business environment. Build your business on your passion and your talents, and both customers and employees will be able to experience the love of what you do, in everything you do.

I believe that it's important for the future that we all play a bigger game doing what we love to do and bringing our gifts and talents to a larger audience. It's no coincidence that there has been an increased success in the number of talent shows appearing on television around the world. The future generation of commerce will be based on finding people's talents and using those talents for good effect and for the better of others. Time and time again, when I work with clients and investigate the gifts that they have, when they start to focus on those gifts and bring them to a wider audience to help others, you could say that miracles begin to happen.

Integrating your natural talents into your business is like putting a better engine into a car. It ran OK before, but the power of the new engine allows the vehicle to perform in ways it never could. In the same way that the new engine affected the car into which it was installed, putting your natural abilities into your business will mean that your life will be less stressful because you will be doing something you love to do. Happiness will be a part of your everyday experience, and you will be making a much bigger and wider contribution to your world and even the world at large. Life will seem effortless and you will get much more enjoyment out of each and every day. You will feel more fulfilled as your natural talents will be sharpened and honed as you use them, and you will be living your life's purpose.

When you have discovered your vision – your purpose in life – and then start to identify your talents, you will begin to realise that each of your talents is there to assist you with carrying out your vision.

The best way I can explain it is that it's like as a soul you decided you had a mission to carry out, a purpose of what you wanted to achieve when you were born, *your vision*, and when you decided upon that vision, you also decided on what experiences and lessons you wanted to have and learn, and the exact tools you would need to carry out your mission, *your gifts and talents*. The only thing is that, in the process of being born, unfortunately you forgot everything. But everything that you needed was there in that neat little package – you. You don't need anything else, you already have everything. But because you forgot, you now have to remember who you truly are. And as you go through life, events and circumstances show up, which when you look back, you realise the reason why those events showed up in the first place and how they were actually helping you to *remember*. You were on the right train track so to speak, but one side of the carriage was running along on the gravel.

The only way you can find your purpose, your vision, is to go within and to connect with your Higher Mind, your Higher Self and your Higher Purpose. Start to identify your gifts and talents and then you will begin to realise how the tools you needed were there all along, and it doesn't cost you any money to use the tools and, in fact, it brings you amazing joy to do so.

No matter what you do in life as a business leader, these are the central pieces of the jigsaw that so many people miss out on. If you are fearful that you are currently running a business, but your true passion is to do something entirely different, don't worry. Your focus should be to deliver the service you are meant to deliver; what you were put here to do, your purpose, what you discover when you connect with your Higher Self, your God within: "Thy will be done" (*The Lord's Prayer*). You and everything else will be taken care of, and you can always maintain your existing business while developing your true passion.

LEADERSHIP OF THE FUTURE

A leader has the vision and conviction that a dream can be achieved. He inspires the power and energy to get it done.
Ralph Lauren

When it comes to leadership, I'm immediately drawn back to a book I read when I was a teenager: George Orwell's *Animal Farm*. It's an amazing book with so many analogies to life and to business contained within it. But the one thing that stood out for me when reading that book all those years ago was one sentence – "power corrupts, and absolute power corrupts absolutely". I've seen so many occasions where employees have been promoted, or people become really successful either with fame or money, and very quickly it 'goes to their head' like a drug. Their ego takes over and their character changes. It might manifest itself in very small nuances. But in time, that person is heading for failure, and inevitably they do fail.

Many times, when I have been involved with helping to turn a company around from a weak bottom line to profitability, the process has involved getting the staff behind the goals and vision of the business – getting them excited about what 'can be'. In most situations when a business is doing poorly, management often tries to sort it out themselves, and a distance develops between staff and management.

Generally, employees actually want to be a part of achieving the goals of the business. They want to feel the challenge of figuring out how to accomplish a mission and to celebrate the victory when a vision is brought into reality. What is good for management and owners also can be good for the employees. The effective businesses of today (and especially of the future) are being built on platforms of collaboration where everyone is involved and can get excited about the process. The 'them and us' scenario needs to disappear from the business vernacular and business environment, so that emotional investment becomes key.

Building a sense of collaboration and oneness starts with looking at the people who work for your company as 'your team' instead of as just 'your employees'. When everyone in a company feels like a part of something bigger than their job, enthusiasm and excitement for what they are doing becomes a part of their daily approach.

They no longer feel like a liability, but will shine as the asset that they truly are meant to be.

And it all starts with you as leader, whether you like it or not. And although businesses are changing in many areas, the traits of a good leader have been pretty consistent for centuries. Laurie Beth Jones in her book *Jesus, CEO* makes the correlation between Jesus' style of leadership and qualities to that of everyday business leaders. In studying Jesus' leadership style, there are three key strengths: self-mastery, action, and relationships. How different would it be to lead a business in the same way as Jesus led his flock? The truth is that the underlying principles are the same. Jesus knew emphatically who he really was and kept in constant contact with God, "Our Father". Knowing who you truly are takes on a completely different meaning, and therefore gives you an insight into how leading a business with spirituality at its core is very much possible.

I could write many pages about the styles and characteristics of leadership. But fundamentally, leadership is about inspiring and motivating your team. It's about your conviction to build a business, a community, a country which is for the better of all concerned. It's about making a difference.

GREAT LEADERS HAVE GREAT VISIONS

They know who they truly are and their core values. They stand fast to their values and build a culture within an organisation where everybody is on the same page, so to speak. They see their vision as a vocation, a calling, a purpose – not of what they should or want to build, but of what they feel needs to be built. Their vision is bigger and greater than themselves. It's for a greater and higher purpose. They are decisive and determined in their decision-making, even if those decisions appear to be at odds to the populace. They know where those decisions fit in to the overall game plan and they want the people around them to exceed their own expectations. True leadership comes from your heart and soul. When you lead from your heart, you are leading from your passion and your drive. It's felt within, not without. When you are leading in this way, you are connecting with other people at a soul level. You engage them in the desire to achieve your vision, your dream. You don't *manage* people, you inspire them to be involved in a higher purpose: to be part of that dream and to be the best they can be.

STEWARD LEADERSHIP

The fundamental understanding to remember as a business leader for the future is that you come to this earth with nothing but your gifts and talents. But you also leave with nothing, except your experiences and lessons learnt and how you have evolved as a soul. All resources, therefore, are at your disposal to use and multiply, not to diminish. The resources ultimately belong to God and are entrusted to you to make use of in order to carry out your purpose, God's purpose. As a Steward Leader, your purpose is to look after the resources you have to hand, to increase them, not to diminish, to develop and to nurture them. Are we looking after our natural resources, our planet, our Mother Earth? When a corporation is extracting resources from Mother Earth, is that corporation looking after and multiplying the natural resources or diminishing them?

For me, it is about using your gifts and your talents to carry out the work you have been called to do. It's about being grateful for the abundance around you, being a steward of and using the resources you have been provided with to maximise the return on those resources, while maintaining the integrity of the original resources you have been provided with. You are given many opportunities to carry this work out, yet if you fail to do so, those resources and opportunities will be given to somebody else who is more caring and can be entrusted with this responsibility and has proven to do so with the resources they have already been given. If you are not able to look after the resources you have been given, why then should you be given more? If you cannot create and manage wealth, why should you be given more wealth to look after and manage, if you have not been successful in looking after the wealth you have been provided with to date?

When building a business for the future, you have to be thinking of building it on the premise of doing business with the world as opposed to dealing with your own local business patch. This involves a simple mind-shift and, rather than dismissing it instantly, start by asking yourself "How could I ...?". Start to do some research to see how other people are operating in a similar field to yourself and see how they are conducting their business globally. New markets are constantly opening as the countries emerge and their people travel around the world to seek new opportunities. Rather than seeing these as threats, determine the cultural differences and see how you can adapt your product or service to meet these new markets.

Businesses of the future will operate more collaboratively both locally and internationally, working with partners in a variety of different countries and backgrounds. By bringing your talents and values together, you will be bringing your speciality to the world. While offering massive opportunities through the wider market, this also brings its difficulties. But thinking along these lines when developing your business will enable you to put the necessary structures in place.

As business leaders, we are here to be of service. Having a focus on how you can improve the lives of others and make a difference in this world is where we can truly achieve what we are here to do and evolve. It is the intention that you hold that is key.

As a business leader; we all have to think, not of ourselves but of what we want to create. We all start somewhere, no matter how small it may appear. Whatever you are in life – a parent, a spouse, a sibling, an employee, a manager, a friend – you are a leader. We are all leaders. Each person you relate to is looking at you as an example. Whether that be a good example or a poor example, they are still observing who you are as an individual. Just the same way as you too are observing other people and seeing how they go through life. We lead by example in everything that we do, be it business, relationships or family. It's not what we say, it's the actions we take, that count.

To be your authentic self, you have to live your life according to your values in every aspect of your life and to start to break down the multiple personas that so many of us display.

When you realise how you are connected to everyone in collective consciousness, you begin to realise the amazing world we live in and how all of us makes a difference. To make a difference in this world, you must first make a difference in yourself. You are a leader.

It is my belief that there are four pillars to steward leadership: integrity, discernment in decisions, culture and ethics. Let's look at each of these elements.

INTEGRITY

To a lot of people, integrity means being honest and abiding by the rules. And while a lot of people aspire to run their business with integrity, the question is do they really?

But integrity for me means having a clear understanding of who you truly are. It's living a life where you are your authentic self, and how you are *integrated* with everybody else and with a Higher Power – a *oneness*. When you truly understand who you are, abiding by the rules becomes immaterial. You begin to operate from a soulful place and, therefore, all your dealings both in business and in your personal life take on a different, deeper meaning. You are then *one*. It still means that you run your business profitably and with purpose, but it becomes much more than *doing* the business and more about *being* the business.

It's not as simple as "Do unto others as you would like done unto you". It's more than that. It's operating from your soul. And all that comes from your soul is love. We are all here to live on one principle and that is love.

How is this relevant to business? It has everything to do with business. When you give love, meaning living with integrity, you receive love, meaning you receive integrity. When you enter your dealings with business and with people with integrity, everybody wins. Yes, sometimes people do not completely operate with integrity and sometimes you might get 'burnt'. However, later in this book, I will discuss how you can begin to trust your gut feelings and begin to easily make the right decisions for you and your business. Therefore, the instances where you may get burnt can be quite limited.

DISCERNMENT

When it comes to making a decision in life or in business, we need to look at the reasons behind why we are acting in a particular way. Or for that matter, why others might be acting in a certain way. We need to look at all sides and know the truth behind our decisions and what motivates them.

Are we making decisions based on securing our own positions, because it's useful to us or it protects us? Or is it to appease others, to comply with the norm, or because we are influenced by another leader? Is there a temptation distracting us from making the right decision? What is our intention? How do you make a decision in life amongst the chaos that goes on around you?

When making decisions, we need to go deep within ourselves to see what is right. We need to connect with our inner selves and see the truth of our decisions. Do our decisions match our values? Who are the stakeholders involved? Are we bowing to pressure from the populace or are we fundamentally doing the right thing? In all our decisions as an individual, there needs to be a deeper understanding and realisation of what we want to achieve by the decisions we make and the impact that those decisions will have. We can only achieve this by having the full information. Then with reflection and connecting with God, we can truly make the right decision. By knowing what the right decision is to make, it then takes courage to do what is right. It's about doing the right thing. That's when a true leader shines.

CULTURE

As a business leader, you are influencing the culture in your organisation. Every aspect of how you live and being true to your values manifests itself in the culture of your organisation. If you are a person of integrity, the culture in your organisation will be integrity. Any company is only as good as its leadership. You can reach the top of your game through your skills, knowledge and expertise. However, when you're leading an organisation, that's when you need to reflect on your values the most, what is important to you and what is the difference you want to make.

The Jesuits use the Latin word *magis*, meaning always something more, something greater. As leaders, we should be striving for something more, something greater. We should be open to change and not be attached to what we have. We are not the position we hold, the car that we drive, the house that we live in or what we possess. We are much more than that. We must reflect on what is within, not with-out.

In your dealings with others – employees, suppliers, customers – examine your interactions and determine your intent. What are you looking to achieve. Will both parties be better off? In negotiations: is the outcome a win-win situation or is the other party losing out?

ETHICS

Over this last decade, as we have watched companies such as Enron collapse and multiple banking institutions fall into bankruptcy and disarray, we are coming to understand that making our businesses better requires much more than just making a profit.

Where at one time, profits were the bottom line for every business and doing better than our competitors was our main goal, the importance of values and ethics and the way we impact our customers, our employees, our communities and our world have now come to the forefront in order for a business to be successful. Therefore, not only do we have to put processes in place that consistently improve our products, production and profitability, we also have to incorporate practices that speak to the core reasons that we are in business.

In simplistic terms, a lack of ethics and good morals was behind the collapse of Enron, various politicians, banks and religious leaders. This can be limited to just a few people in key positions or can be endemic to a business team.

In other words, a business that is formed and run without being true to stated core values that are in alignment for the benefit of all concerned is like a house being built on ground that cannot support it. The popular parable of the wise man who built his house upon the rock sums it up perfectly, as opposed to the house that was built on sand. Your values are your cornerstone to building firm foundations for your business and your life. If your life or business is not in alignment with your core values or those core values are not in alignment for the benefit of all concerned, then at some point it will have an impact on the success of your business. In other words, a business (or a life for that matter) that is built without using the strength of core values and ethics for the benefit of all will not have the strength to stand up against the challenges and storms that are a natural rhythm of life and business.

This is where the core values that we identified earlier in this book come into play. Are honesty, integrity, and honour part of your values? These values need to be integrated into every part of your business, and employees, customers and suppliers should be able to easily recognise them.

FedEx is a good example of a company that became successful by incorporating values into its day-to-day operations and it continues to follow those values as the company changes, grows and make things better. The values that are followed and integrated into everything FedEx does are:

- Valuing people and promoting diversity.

- A positive spirit that puts customers at the heart of everything they do.

- Innovation that constantly improves the way they work and live.

- Integrity that is integrated into every part of their operations.

- A sense of responsibility for safe and healthy environments in the communities in which they do business and constantly striving to earn the loyalty of their people, customers and investors.

In 10 of the last 11 years, FedEx has been honoured as one of *Fortune* magazine's '100 Best Companies to Work For' and consistently ranks in *Fortune*'s list of the 'World's Most Admired Companies'. FedEx attributes these awards and recognition to the "absolutely, positively" spirit of the men and women who "make FedEx what it is. FedEx was founded on a people-first philosophy, where respect for all people is a fundamental value and everyday business practice".

FedEx is an excellent example of how knowing what you value and then integrating those things into your business will act as a set of guiding principles that will not only help you in your decisions, but will set a standard for your company.

And even though ethics, morals and putting value in people seem to be 'new ways of thinking', there are many companies that have implemented these policies quietly from the very beginning and are continuing to experience success.

Toyota Motor Corporation is a good example. On 30 October, 1935, the Toyota Precepts were published, and these precepts (over the years and up to this present time) have "played the role of a spiritual support for employees as the principles of the company". These are the Toyota precepts as written in 1935, which are still followed to this day:

1. Be contributive to the development and welfare of the country by working together, regardless of position, in faithfully fulfilling your duties.

2. Be ahead of the times through endless creativity, inquisitiveness and pursuit of improvement.

3. Be practical and avoid frivolity.

4. Be kind and generous, strive to create a warm, homelike atmosphere.

5. Be reverent, and show gratitude for things great and small in thought and deed.

When events arose for the Toyota corporation in early 2010 regarding faults with their vehicles, their approach was one of self-admittance to those failures, openness with the global public and an honesty as to where the failures materialised. Contrast the approach that was taken by Toyota to that taken by BP Oil in mid-2010 following the oil-spill disaster off the Gulf of Mexico. Two distinctive approaches were taken by each corporation.

More and more companies are embracing spiritual principles as they strive to make it better on all levels of their organisations and, by doing so, they are experiencing growth and improvement in every area of business.

NYNEX Corporation established an Office of Ethics and Business Conduct to encourage employees to live by a set of core values: quality, ethics and caring for the individual. This new focus led to increases in profits, productivity and product and service quality, as this affected how the company is perceived by customers and stakeholders.

When you strive to be the best and to improve continuously the way you do things, what you are doing in effect is making your business more efficient and more profitable, while respecting the people who help you succeed and the resources you use in the process of providing your products or services. Consumers are watching every step that businesses take, and are supporting principled businesses that exhibit a sense of responsibility along with a desire for profit.

In his book, *The New Entrepreneurs,* Michael Ray, professor at Stanford University's Graduate School of Business, states:

> *The real heroes of today are people dealing with the challenges of a world in chaotic transition. They know the difficulty and suffering that is part of this world. But they also have full faith in their inner creativity and spirit with its infinite intuition, will, joy, strength, and compassion. They know that the job and promise of life is taking these inner qualities and bringing them forth in a constant quest for the highest for themselves and everyone around them.*

In most areas of business, an owner's IQ (Intelligence Quotient), or their abilities with mathematical and verbal skills, plays a strong part in how well they understand and master the techniques and strategies that help align them for success. With people management, however, an owner's EQ (Emotional Quotient) or their ability to interact and relate to others, and their SQ (Spiritual Quotient) or their inner wisdom and capacity for compassion, are beginning to play a strong part in the success they experience.

In fact, in some companies today, and in many companies in the future, SQ will play a much bigger role as companies are designed with less emphasis on 'managing people' and more emphasis on trusting the individual to set their own objectives and be accountable for the outcomes. By removing the concept of 'policing', a whole layer of expensive hierarchy is automatically dissolved, freeing up the potential for people's inherent leadership qualities to grow instead. We see this, for example, in the way many businesses facilitate employees in remotely working one or two days a week so long as they are contactable.

However, the truth is that a majority of business leaders are not yet ready to make the transition from the rigid control of the past to a 'company without borders' concept. Yet, owners and management are discovering that, when warmth, encouragement, support and trust are integrated into all people interactions, when this permeates down from the top layers of a company to the bottom, employees become the strongest tool they have for being able to turn visions and goals into reality.

At present, there is a spiritual awakening happening around the globe. And in order to fully engage their individual spiritual quotients, leaders are learning to trust their own intuition and spirituality in all facets of running their business, and these traits are being brought to the forefront where employees are concerned. Many companies are now taking a 'team' approach, where management and employees work together as a unit to achieve the visions and goals for the company as a whole.

More and more businesses of the future will be built using an open and collaborative approach to solving problems and servicing the marketplace, where the benefit will be to the greater community. The rise in independent business owners will continue to soar, which will enable people to specialise in their areas of expertise according to their core values, gifts and talents. In this way, business can be done in a global marketplace. This is where business is evolving to. Embracing these changes now will enable your company to get the best of the best for your business and extend your capabilities of what can be achieved.

Whether they work in your office and live in your community or work virtually and live on the other side of the world, thoughtfully managing every member of your team and leading them in this new way will help take your vision and dream and turn it into a profitable reality.

Imagine the scenario where what is being discussed in this book transcends to your employees and the people who work with you. Imagine a situation where each individual engages their gifts and talents, understands who they truly are, their connection with God, operating using their intuition, and are matched with your values and all are working together to develop a business that is for the greater good of the wider community? What would that be like? Is it possible?

I believe it is. It all starts with you as a business leader, defining your true purpose and pursuing it with the collaboration of all the people involved with you. Instead of discussing "Why not?", what if we start by discussing "How can we ...?".

As a leader, you lead yourself according to your authentic self, your integrated self. When you lead yourself, others will follow. Be true to yourself.

VALUE YOUR
INTUITION

Listen to your intuition. It will tell you everything you need to know.
Anthony J. D'Angelo

When I look back on my own career and what I have done in my own business, every single time I tapped into my intuition, my Higher Mind, I would always get an indication as to when I was to move on from what I was doing in my career and in my business. I then would start to develop a new service or a different way of delivering my service to clients, and invariably I was right every time. Many times I discussed my plans with colleagues and friends and, every time, I was told I was mad! It wouldn't work! It's not the way things are done! Would I not stay where I was? Yet every time, each new pursuit worked out for me and rewarded me handsomely.

The problem for many people is that we think too much. We over-analyse and we create our own fears. As human beings, we are the only species that can imagine our own death. The pictures we can create in our own minds are so powerful that they either can paralyse us from action, or motivate us to move mountains.

With the turmoil we have seen in recent years and the regular news of negative events, it's difficult to maintain our sense of focus and what we want to achieve in life and in business. When all we see around us is doom and gloom, then it's hard to get motivated to do anything. We all get to a point in our lives where we feel totally alone and we don't see any way out. Then the thoughts of taking what we see as the easy way out begin to occupy our minds. We only see darkness, not light. We don't see hope, just despair. We feel nobody understands us and that we're the only ones in this world in this position and that nobody cares. We feel that everybody would be better off without us being in this world and it wouldn't make a difference if we were gone. Such feelings are so real that we think that taking what we see as the easy route out of this lifetime is the only road to take.

However, that easy route is not easy in any manner or means. The despair that is left behind is boundless. The impact of feelings, questions and loss on others is so profound that they become indescribable. However, if you take on board what I put forward in this book, in its entirety, you will never ever feel alone again in your life.

FILTERING

In some ways, we have to take control of our mind. Through our five senses (seeing, hearing, smelling, tasting and touching), we take in millions of pieces of data every second. With this amount of data, we have to filter some of it out. But equally, we also need to process a lot of it in order to determine what to do at that point in time.

Look at it in this way, your internal filters are like a sieve. What the sieve doesn't let through its filters is what you really want to capture. With your mind, you are filtering all the data you receive and discarding what doesn't fit in with your filtering system. However, what you might be discarding at any point in time may be a diamond in the rough which is just waiting for you to polish in order to see its true potential.

We filter in various ways. First, we automatically *delete information* that we receive if it's not relevant to us. If we choose to make it relevant, then we take more cognisance of that element of information that we are processing. Take, for example, when you buy something new for yourself, like a new car. Prior to buying it, you may not have noticed other people driving a similar car to the one you have just purchased. However, pretty soon after you buy your new car, you start to notice other people with the same car and same colour as you. Were they always there before? Of course they were, but the information wasn't relevant to you at the time, so you automatically deleted it.

The other way we filter information out is that *we generalise.* If you have been driving a car for a number of years, I'm sure there have been times when you were driving home from work not even *thinking* about what you were doing to drive the car, whether it be changing the gears, or observing what was around you, and before you know it, you are at your home. The data you were receiving at that time wasn't necessary to give it your full attention, so you filtered it out.

Then come our *values*. I have discussed how important your values are. If you receive information to your brain that is not in sync with your values, you will dismiss it as it's not important to you. If, for example, spirituality is a high value for you, then you will observe spirituality in everything that you do. If family is a high value for you, then everything that you do and observe will be in correlation with activities around family. If wealth is a high value to you, then everything you do will be associated with the activity of creating and managing wealth.

We then filter based on our *beliefs*. We all grow up with a belief system, whether you like it or not. One person may believe that it's hard to be successful in business (I'm here to tell you that it doesn't have to be!), while others may believe that money is evil or that you have to be ruthless in business in order to succeed. Take, for example, a child who was bitten by a dog when he or she was really young. Most likely, that child would grow up believing that all dogs were dangerous, would stay away from dogs and probably not ever get a dog as a pet. This interpretation is a limiting belief. All dogs are not dangerous. But this is the belief that person has.

We all have beliefs that hold us back in life and in business. A typical one I come across is that 'all' sales people are sleazy and are out to 'pull a fast one'. But when you're running your own business, sales is an integral part of your business if it is to be successful. If you believe sales people are sleazy, then you're going to have a pretty hard time selling on behalf of your own business.

All your interpretations of what you believe to be true are perceptions. It's what you understand it to be. It's your view of the world. You've got to question yourself where those beliefs came from. But the really important question is whether the beliefs that we hold are serving us well. If you have limiting beliefs that are preventing you in achieving your vision, then the best thing to do is to start removing them. Those limiting beliefs can be removed. It's all perception. What beliefs do you think are holding you back?

When the information we have received has gone through each of these filters, we are guided then by our *attitudes*. Whether you are positive or negative, easygoing, or committed, your attitudes will determine what you will do with the information.

We then will compare the remaining data to our *memories* to find a similar situation to the one we find ourselves in right now, to see what the outcome was in the past. We will determine whether the memory is a good one or a bad one. Nobel Prize-winner Ivan Pavlov's experiment with dogs comes to mind here. Pavlov became interested in studying reflexes when he saw that the laboratory dogs drooled without the proper stimulus. Although no food was in sight, their saliva still dribbled. It turned out that the dogs were reacting to lab coats. Every time the dogs were served food, the person who served the food was wearing a lab coat. Therefore, the dogs reacted as if food was on its way whenever they saw a lab coat. In a series of experiments, Pavlov then tried to figure out how these phenomena were linked. For example, he struck a bell when the dogs were fed. If the bell was sounded in close association with their meal, the dogs learnt to associate the sound of the bell with food. After a while, at the mere sound of the bell, they responded by drooling.

How often do we discount new information based on our experiences or memories of our past? Whatever beliefs or memories we have, both good and bad, they affect the decisions we make and how we react in a given situation. We're reacting in much the same way as the dogs reacted to the sound of the bell. We're programmed to react in a particular way. Our memories are our perception of what happened in a particular event. While some of us may have a positive perception of an event, someone else may have a negative perception of the same event. These perceptions change how you will decide in a similar future event.

Take a simple example of a bad experience you had in a country you visited. Because of that experience, you may not go to that country ever again. Your perception is that it's not a great country to visit and that you should be cautious of the people there. However, this is your perception based on a memory you have. You might go to that same country again and have a completely different and positive experience. When we react to something, we are reacting in the same way as the dogs in Pavlov's experiment, based on a memory. Where else in your life are you limiting yourself based on the memories that you have? If you didn't have those memories, how would you approach a similar situation?

The last of the filters is our own self-talk or our *ego*: the person that is within us who tells us everything that is bad about us or what we cannot achieve. Dr. Wayne Dyer puts it nicely when he stated that ego is just an acronym for "Edging God Out".

Our self-talk will affect our feelings and put us into an emotional state, be it positive or negative. If the emotional state is positive, then great. If it's negative, then we will make decisions based on a lesser part of our being. By that I mean we make decisions based on a perception of ourselves that is not positive, from a place where we have low self-belief, low confidence, low self-esteem. It is our map of the world: our own micro-world. Our beliefs, our perceptions, and a belief that we are not connected to God. With this tiny map of the world that we put ourselves in, our decisions then become tiny. However, all the decisions we make and the actions we take have consequences. While in a positive state, we will make better decisions. When making a decision, what is the self-talk that is going on in your head? What is the intention of your decision?

Our decisions then will determine what actions we will take, either positive or negative. As a result of these actions, obviously there will be an outcome or a result. The results we achieve then will determine what we observe and allow to be processed by our brain.

Therefore, it's a never-ending cycle of what we observe, to what we process, to what results we get. The key is to make sure you master that process and feed the 'mind-processing loop' with the correct information. Therefore, you have to learn to control your conscious mind and your subconscious mind.

ENGAGE YOUR SUBCONSCIOUS MIND

By creating a vision and a focused mindset, successful entrepreneurs are able to engage their conscious minds as well as their subconscious minds, which according to Napoleon Hill:

... draws upon the forces of Infinite Intelligence for the power with which it voluntarily transmutes one's desires into their physical equivalent, making use always of the most practical media by which this end may be accomplished.

In other words, create a strong, focused mindset, believe that you can accomplish what you set out to do, pay attention to your intuition, and move forward with a purposeful goal in mind.

Napoleon Hill's book is titled *Think & Grow Rich*. It's through our thinking that we achieve success. But if it was that easy, why doesn't everybody do it? It's easy in theory but more difficult in execution, because you have to stay focused and clear on what your vision, your intention and your purpose is. Many people jump around with their thoughts and actions, never having one clear goal of what they want to accomplish. Like the sunlight through a magnifying glass that is focused on a spot on a wooden log, focusing your thoughts, actions, and behaviours on your vision and what you intend to accomplish will catch flame to your life.

I've seen so many people jump from one idea to the next, all the time thinking that the new idea will make them rich. They get distracted with the latest idea and it becomes as attractive as a new shiny object. You have to stay focused. When you've put your attention on something, follow it through. Everything starts to come into being when your attention is focused. When you change onto something else, everything else now has to realign to what you want. So stay focused.

With your attention focused on your vision, your mindset supporting your focus and your subconscious mind linking you to your God, an unlimited source of wisdom and inspiration, you will begin to notice that opportunities you never thought existed will begin to appear. You will start to achieve success like never before and things will begin to run much more smoothly. You will achieve a lot more each day and you will become happier and more self-fulfilled.

Have you ever noticed how some people in the same industry are successful and others are not? What separates the great from the mediocre is that the great create a focused mindset and tap into an unlimited source that very few understand.

One of the most powerful parts of you is your subconscious mind. But the difficulty lies in harnessing its power and communicating with your subconscious mind or your intuition. You may know this better as your 'gut feeling' or a 'sixth sense'. Your intuition is like a compass that will always point you in the right direction. Because our conscious mind only works on a small percentage of the information we take in through all our senses, it's limited in the information it has and, therefore, in the decisions it can make. Your subconscious mind, however, takes in everything and, therefore, is better placed to guide you.

We are all on a path, whether you like it or not. We are part of a much bigger plan than you can even imagine. We all can succeed at what it is we want to do, even if it's not in sync with the path we are supposed to be on. However, would it not make a lot more sense to be on the right path, doing what we are supposed to be doing, and doing what we love? We would achieve far greater things in our life as a result, and far more easily than you think possible.

With my clients, I use the analogy of 'the feather, the brick and the truck'. Throughout our life, we get hints and gentle nudges to help us make the right decisions that move us along our paths. These might come in the way of intuitive flashes, eureka moments, inspired thoughts and such like. They are gentle nudges, much like the effect of a feather brushing against your skin. The unaware see these 'feathers' simply as ideas that they will act upon at some stage but generally they forget about them.

Then there's the 'brick'. These nudges are more severe than the 'feather', as you can imagine. An instance might arise in your life that somehow forces you to take notice, make a decision and correct your course of action. We can all survive 'bricks', even though they might be painful at the time. With the work that I do, I'm usually the 'brick'. Through working with people, I discover what they are supposed to be doing, what their purpose is, and I guide them as much as is possible onto that path. A 'brick' also might appear in the form of an enforced career change, a temporary sickness, the loss of a big contract or a change in market conditions. Bricks are survivable without too much disruption but may appear as a significant inconvenience. These are all choice points in our life.

However, if we're still not on our path, our purpose or doing what we need to do, then the 'truck' comes along. You can imagine the truck! You may or may not survive the 'truck'. This can be when everything is stripped away from us, relationships, our business, our health ... but, all the time, we have a choice. We can recognise it for what it is and amend the path we are taking or we can give up. When I was faced with the 'truck', I had to make a choice: continue to be here on this earth or follow my purpose.

You see, before every breakdown, there's a breakthrough. It's at these times that you have to volunteer your conscious mind and listen to your intuition, follow it and know that it will lead you to where you need to be.

A number of clients have come to me when they were at the brink of self-destruction. Each time, I've told them what they need to do. Some have taken heed and, at that choice point, have taken my advice and amended their course. Others, unfortunately, have not and multiple disasters have hit them. Still others take on board what I tell them, but continue down the same course regardless, before finally making a decision to change in line with what I outlined to them in the first place, to find that everything turns around for them with very little effort.

In my view, we've a role to play, a purpose. A lot of us play that role with exquisite precision, without even being aware of it. Others struggle, however, and part of the work that I do is to help them be on their right path. In every desperate situation you might find yourself in, consider it as a choice point for you. Which way do you want to proceed? Always listen to your intuition, ask for guidance, connect with God within, and you will never go wrong.

There are two aspects when it comes to your mind:

- Taking control of your conscious mind.
- Tapping into your Higher Mind or your intuition.

Typically, your mind is referred to as your conscious mind and your subconscious mind. Your conscious mind is the *thinking* part of your brain, where all logical analysis is conducted. Its whole purpose is to keep you alive. Without you being alive, it doesn't exist. Therefore, it keeps you safe and in your comfort zone. Your subconscious mind is that part of you that makes sure the blood is pumped around your body, keeps your heart beating and chooses what muscles need to be coordinated in order to carry out a movement – without you even having to think about it! Millions of functions are being controlled by your subconscious mind every minute of every day without you even having to do anything.

Your mind is always working on obtaining a solution to a problem you present to it. I'm sure you have had the situation where you've gone to bed trying to figure a problem out but just can't seem to get the solution. Once you awake, a flash of inspiration comes to you which *gives* you the solution you were looking for all along. The main reason for this is that, during sleep, you have allowed the brain to quieten and enabled it to give you the information you were looking for. We go around all day with so much *noise* that we cannot hear ourselves *think*.

These instances when you get a flash of inspiration are your gold dust and are the way your Higher Mind connects with you to give you the steps to move forward. Many successful people have a notepad beside their bed so that, when they get these intuitive flashes of inspiration, they can take note of them. Some successful people even have notepads throughout their house, office, car, literally everywhere. Why? Because they know the value of these intuitive flashes. Most people, however, get the flash of inspiration but then don't do anything with it. They believe they can remember it and will take note of it at some future point. But opportunities aren't lost, they're just passed on to somebody else who takes action on them instead.

These flashes come from your Higher Consciousness, your God. They are always right. They are always the correct course of action for you to take, at that very moment. If you leave it until some future date, it will be too late and, therefore, will not give you the results you desire. The important thing is that you need to take action immediately. The difficult part is in determining whether it is our imagination or our intuition. How you develop your intuition is through meditation.

Sometimes, when we get these flashes, we start to rationalise each one of them. We start to look at the pros and cons of taking the action attaching to a particular intuitive flash. This is where our conscious mind is operating and taking over. This is where so many go wrong.

The more you develop your intuition, the more inspiration you will receive.

If you can imagine being in a crowded room at a party, where you're standing in one corner of the room and there's another person in the diagonal opposite corner of the room trying to communicate to you. However, with all the noise of people talking and music in the background, it's really difficult to hear that person. But if we quieten everything down, turn the music off and get all the people to stay quiet, and even turn our own thoughts off, then we would be well able to hear that person speak and what they are trying to communicate to us.

Your inner soul, your intuition, your subconscious mind is trying to communicate to you all the time. You just can't *hear* it. All you have to do is quieten your mind and body in order to be able to listen and communicate. Be still, be silent.

By meditating regularly, you allow your mind to quieten and enable it to connect with your Higher Mind. Through meditation, you develop your intuitive side, the gut feeling side of you. Most successful people in business always act on their gut feeling. When you act on your intuition, you are acting on your true self.

The more you act on your true self, the more you will be living a life of authenticity and success in the true sense.

When it comes to bringing innovation into your business, there are the practical steps and systems to be taken like brainstorming, creative thinking, lateral thinking. These work extremely well when operating with a team of people within your organisation. However, in my view, the most powerful form of innovation is using the power within yourself, your Higher Consciousness.

QUIETEN THE MIND

This leads me on to meditative creative contemplation, where you actively quieten the mind to enable you to think creatively, and where you will get your greatest source of imagination.

Thomas Edison used this process regularly in his work. He would meditate in his chair with two ball-bearings in the palms of his hands and allow himself to drift deeper and deeper. The moment he reached a deep state, the ball-bearings would fall onto a steel plate on the floor below his hands and he would wake up.

Accordingly, he was able to calibrate the point between full consciousness and self-hypnosis where he knew the great belt of creativity and ingenuity lay. That is where his neurology lit up – like a light bulb!

For your business to be successful into the future, you need to adopt a new way of thinking and building. Successful people have learned to listen to and trust their intuition. More importantly, they act on these flashes of inspiration with immediate action because they have faith in where it comes from. Having a powerful mindset is your path to connecting with your God. Stay fast to your vision without changing your mind.

You truly can have all the desires you want, but first you have to learn what your true desires really are. When you identify what you really want to achieve, you have engaged your passion which in turn brings about what you want. Because we don't determine what we really want in life, our mind keeps changing from one thing to another. With this constant mind-changing, it's impossible to really succeed in business.

At times, we need to get out of our own way. We *think* too much. We need to stop *thinking* and start listening to our soul voice, that voice within us all that is trying to guide you in life. When you understand, appreciate and believe who you truly are, then your desires will become reality. This is when you are truly evolving as a soul towards your greater self.

EVERYDAY
SUCCESS HABITS

Successful people are simply those with success habits.
Brian Tracy

Every business leader experiences from time to time the silent, empty vacuum in which our own doubts can grow to be monstrous and our own opinion, however wrong-headed, is the only one available. Unless you have a clear sense of personal direction, the loss of association and interaction can be deeply disturbing.

When planning how you are going to structure your business, make sure you take yourself into account. It's fine and well organising the premises, the equipment, the staff, the customers, yet the most important individual in any organisation is the business leader – yourself. You have to make sure your needs and wants are being looked after. If you don't invest in yourself, your business will suffer. Ensure you build into your business structure, or the corporate environment you work in, how you are going to take care of yourself. More importantly, how you are going to take time out for yourself.

I have already put forward how important it is to connect with your God. If you are always involved in the business, how are you going to be able to maintain your connection? God is always there waiting for you to ask for what you want. In times of crisis, God is the one person you need to be turning to. Except we forget at the times when it's needed the most. We look externally to other sources like the economy, to the politicians for answers, leadership and guidance. And yet we don't harness our most important faculty, our mind, and we don't tap into our Higher Consciousness for help to guide us on the exact path we should follow. So whichever way you structure your business, make sure you structure your ability to take time out for yourself to connect with God. The following are some elements you might consider incorporating in your life.

UNDERSTAND CAUSE AND EFFECT

Cause is what makes something happen; effect is what happens. If you choose to be optimistic, that is the cause. The positive impact it has on your life is the effect. It's important to understand that every choice you make has an effect – some are short-term and some end up being long-term. By understanding this, you are able to consciously stay on the cause side of the equation of life, which gives you the power and ability to change your environment and your life. Our thoughts cause us to act, and our actions are the causes that manifest into our life and our businesses.

If you choose to be on the 'effect' side, you are accepting that your life is controlled by external forces, environments, and people. You are surrendering your control to others. You begin to make excuses and reasons why things aren't happening for you – people won't buy your product *because* the price is too high, there's no business *because* nobody has any cash to spend, we've been cursed *because* every time we seem to move ahead in our business, there's somebody there waiting to knock us – and the list goes on and on. These are all external influences. You've handed control over to other people. Eliminate excuses from your life completely. They don't exist. Not everybody in the world thinks your product is priced too high. Not everybody in the world has no money to spend. You haven't been cursed, you've cursed yourself.

By choosing to be on the 'cause' side of things, you take control over your own life and what you want showing up. The rich and successful believe that they themselves create their life, whereas many of the poor believe they are a victim of their circumstances. They blame other people and circumstances for their situation, and they try to justify why they are where they are. You must take responsibility for everything in your life. I mean *everything* in your life.

If your life isn't showing up as you would like it, then it's your responsibility to go change it. Sometimes, it may be hard and really tough to accomplish, but how much do you want it? What are you making a higher priority? By taking responsibility and being on the cause side of life, you then have the power to do something about your life that will change the effect.

We all have a life story to tell. How our parents didn't love us, or we lost a job, or we weren't born into a rich family. Whatever it is, we have to get over it. It was probably the best thing that could have happened to you. Now you know what that experience is like, you don't have to experience it again. Life is about gaining experiences.

Choose to be on the cause side of the life equation and give yourself that power to have control over your own destiny. What are you going to do differently from this day forward? If you could change one thing, what would it be? What's stopping you from achieving what you want? You are the only one stopping yourself.

UNDERSTAND YOUR CONSCIOUS AND SUBCONSCIOUS MIND

The experiences you have with your five senses (seeing, hearing, smelling, tasting and touching) are perceived by your conscious mind, and then stored away as a memory into your subconscious mind. The subconscious mind is like a computer where data is stored, and it's also the connection or doorway between your conscious mind and your Higher Power.

As I discussed earlier in the book, we take in a massive amount of data every second through our conscious mind, but then this is filtered through our mental sieve via our limiting beliefs and the programmes we run in our brain. The subconscious mind, however, has the ability to take in all information. It has the further ability to process that information and communicate it to your conscious mind through intuition or gut feelings or through senses, feelings, or other manifestations in your body. The more you clear the channels between your conscious mind and your subconscious mind, then the more you are able to get the answers to guide you on your path.

Consider this as your connection with your God, the all-knowing. You can begin to achieve this through meditation, through scripting, and through sitting in silence. To get a deeper understanding of your subconscious mind, perhaps begin by reading *The Power of Your Subconscious Mind* by Joseph Murphy.

VISUALISE YOUR DREAM

A daily habit of visualising your goals as having been achieved will bring all the forces of your subconscious mind into play.

Many people use 'vision boards' or pictures to represent what it looks like when they have achieved their goals. A 'vision board' is like a notice board which has a collage of all the pictures that represent the things you want in your life. For example, it might have pictures of the kind of office building you want to have for your business, or a picture representing each of your sites around the world.

What's important is that all of your senses are brought into play in order to bring your burning desire towards achieving your goals. Whether you want to open a bakery shop or a global corporation supplying product around the world, it all starts with your vision and what it looks like in your mind's eye. Remember Bill Gates' vision was to have a computer in every home. You can achieve whatever you set your mind to. Your subconscious mind has no concept of time. Therefore, when you visualise your vision, you are bringing all the life energy of your subconscious mind into play in order to move you closer to achieving your vision.

Many books have been written that explain the importance of visualisation and how to visualise; however, a lot of these books don't emphasise the importance of taking action. Visualising your end goal alone is not sufficient. You must take action. You will be guided as to what action to take based on your intuition.

Do you know what your business will look like when you're finished? What images can you bring together for your vision board to help you with visualising your future?

SET YOUR GOALS

Your business strategy will help create the milestones to mark what needs to be accomplished in order to achieve your vision. Very few people set goals for themselves or for their business, and even fewer do anything about achieving those goals. If you had your life to live over again, would you achieve more than what you've achieved so far? It's about living a purposeful life.

When setting your goals, set achievable goals, but goals that stretch you. The problem is not that we set our goals too high, it's the fact that we set our goals too low. So set ambitious goals. Don't worry about how you're going to achieve your goals. The 'how' will always be looked after once you commit to your goals.

Then you need to regularly review your goals and keep asking yourself, "What is the one thing I am doing today that is moving me closer to my goal?". Whatever that action is that needs to be taken, just do it. Don't procrastinate. If you maintain this level of focus, you will achieve your goals far sooner than you expect.

Now this is quite different from business goals, where a project might be broken down into its constituent parts and each department in the company is involved in achieving the business goal. However, this type of goal-setting is more personal but there are elements that can still be drawn into your business goals. It's best to set your goals in the present tense, because your subconscious mind has no concept of time. When you state your goals in the present tense, you are creating a tension between what currently exists and what you want to bring into existence. Your subconscious mind will use this tension to assist you in achieving your goals and bringing them into existence.

Next, set a reward for when you achieve your goal, and this can be more powerful than the goal itself. From a corporate perspective, you might set a reward of a short holiday for your department in an exotic location for when you achieve your goal of launching a new product range, for example. Your subconscious mind likes getting rewarded just as much as you do yourself!

FOCUS ON ONE THING

Keep your vision in mind as you move forward with the steps that you need to take to create it into reality. Always look towards the future and see the possibilities, while doing what has to be done each day. Be a 'long-term thinker,' and ensure that what you are doing today is leading you one step closer to your 'end goal'.

Don't have your thoughts jump around different projects and goals you want to achieve. Take one at a time and stay focused on that one thing. As I referred to in one of the earlier chapters, if you focus a magnifying glass on a piece of wood with the sunlight coming through it like a laser beam, it will soon catch light. If you keep moving the magnifying glass around, you are making it extremely difficult, if not impossible, for the piece of wood to catch fire. Keep this level of laser focus on your goals all the time until you have made it into reality.

TAKE TIME OUT EACH DAY

Spend some time each day in thought and quiet contemplation, allowing thoughts and ideas to flow from your subconscious mind. That's why it's so important as a business leader not to be working *in* the business the whole time, but to be working *on* the business.

You have only one role when running a business no matter the size, and that is to develop and grow the business. That's it, nothing else. Without taking time out each day to explore possibilities, you are stymieing the growth of your business.

This is also a time to become aware of the presence of God in your thoughts, in everything that you do, and in the people you meet. Review what has happened in your day so far, and where God was calling you. Reflect on how you responded in these situations. With that reflection in mind, ask yourself what you will try to do differently for the rest of the day. How will you respond differently to people and circumstances? How will you become more aware of the presence of God in everything that you do?

Now ask yourself how you can build this 'time out' into your daily routine.

HAVE FUN

Enjoy each day and each person, experience, and opportunity that comes into your life. Be serious in your intention, but not in your attitude. Life is supposed to be fun. You are supposed to have fun as part of your journey through this lifetime. Make sure you build it in. There are a multitude of ways you can build fun into your life and into your business.

Apart from the physical and biological impact of having fun where endorphins are released into the body, you are building on your motivation to move your business forward. Life is not about the destination, it's about the journey you take.

MEDITATE

The power of meditation cannot be underestimated. Apart from reducing your stress levels and allowing your brain to get much-needed rest, it's also powerful in developing your creativity, your focus and intuitive side, and enabling you to connect with your Higher Mind. Personally, I do Transcendental Meditation each day. It allows my mind to be clear and more focused.

While it may appear that nothing has changed in your world after doing meditation, the effect that you have is that everything has changed. You view the world differently.

What would you do to become less stressed, more focused, and more creative? Meditation doesn't cost you anything to do, so what's stopping you from doing it? Would it surprise you to know that nearly every successful business person meditates regularly? It's because they understand the power of meditation.

SCRIPT REGULARLY

Writing is one of the mediums by which your subconscious mind can bypass your conscious mind and bring new thoughts, ideas, and concepts to your attention. So take time to reflect and ponder the questions you want answered and record all your thoughts on paper. When scripting to access the subconscious mind, you don't 'think' about what you are writing. You just write whatever comes into your mind, whatever it is. When you allow yourself to let go and 'stop thinking', you will get to a point where something else takes over. Your style of writing might change or even the language that you use will appear to be different. Sometimes, the thoughts that will be coming into your mind will be flowing so fast that your hand will not be able to keep up with the speed of writing. This is when you have connected with your Higher Mind. Get out of your own way and stop *thinking*. Simply get a journal and a pen that you like writing with, and write whatever thoughts come into your mind. No matter how trivial the thought might be, write it down.

If you have a question that you want answered, write it down and then write whatever comes into your mind. Even if the thoughts don't relate to the question you want answered, write them down. Don't sit there pondering about what you might write, you should be writing all the time. Your conscious mind has millions of thoughts, so you will have plenty to write. While you may not get any answers to your questions at first, through regular meditation you will begin to unlock your subconscious mind, allowing a flow of information to come through.

It's best that you do scripting first thing in the morning when you awake. This is when you will get your most precious insights.

WATCH THE WORDS YOU USE

Be mindful of the words you speak ... make sure they are more about what you want to create than what you don't want to create. Words are powerful.

In *The Four Agreements,* author Don Miguel Ruiz reminds us:

The word is not just a sound or a written symbol. The word is a force; it's the power you have to express and communicate, to think and thereby to create the events in your life ... the word is the most powerful tool you have as a human; it's the tool of magic. But like a sword with two edges, your word can create the most beautiful dream, or your word can destroy everything around you.

That's why affirmations work so well for many people. Your words are extremely powerful and have a force all by themselves. The spoken word has more power than the *thought* word. That is to say, if you are going to use affirmations, speak them aloud.

Japanese author Masaru Emoto carried out research on the effect of our thoughts and speech on water crystals in order to prove this concept of the power of words. His findings are fascinating and are shown in the different shapes that water crystals take on as a result of various words that are used. By doing an Internet search for Emoto's work, you will be able to read for yourself and see images of the effect of words on water crystals.

Be mindful of the words that you use, whether words of anger or disrespect towards somebody or words you use to describe what you want in life. For example, I recently had a conversation with a business owner who said, "I just want to be comfortable and have enough to live on ...". If that's what you want, then that's what you'll get.

Why not want and achieve more? Look at all the good you can do in the world when you have more. It's not about the money. It's about what you can do with the money to make your community a better place and make a difference in other people's lives. When you have more, do you think others will have less? Do you think there is a scarcity in the world and, therefore, you shouldn't want more? Where does this belief come from? Start to observe the words you use and those of people around you.

HAVE AN ATTITUDE OF GRATITUDE

In her book, *Gratitude: A Way of Life,* Louise Hay says:

> *Gratitude is not the result of things that happen to us, it's an attitude we cultivate by practice. The more we are thankful for, the more we will find to be thankful for.*

An attitude of gratitude is essential for staying connected with a Higher Source because gratitude keeps us in a positive frame of mind, which impacts our thought processes and overall interactions as well. It keeps us in a 'love' space.

If you were to give a present to your partner each day, and didn't receive any acknowledgement or gratitude in return, how long do you think you would continue to give your partner presents? If you are not grateful for the positives that you receive in your life every day, why would you be entitled to receive more?

Start by keeping a diary or a notepad beside your bed, and each night write down all the things you are grateful for in your life and the happenings throughout the day that you are grateful for. This will do two things: it will change your outlook on life as you begin to observe all the things that are good in your life, and it also will imbed in your subconscious mind as you go to sleep all the positives that are in your life. Then, when you wake up in the morning, you're waking up having reviewed the positives and things you are grateful for, and therefore will change how you view the world that day. It's a lot better than having all the negative thoughts going around your head before you fall asleep. Which would you rather have?

However, when you understand who you truly are, and that God is within you, you can only but be grateful for everything in your life and truly see everything that is around you. All you crave for is that connection, deep within each of us, that unconditional love that we look elsewhere for in all the wrong places. And when we experience this love, you crave for it even more. It's an overwhelming love like no other.

PRACTICE FORGIVENESS

Being willing to forgive people is essential for being able to connect with your Higher Source. Anger is a negative emotion and negative emotions keep us away from being able to connect with our intuition and Higher Power. "Forgive us our trespasses, as we forgive those who trespass against us" (*The Lord's Prayer*).

Practice forgiveness regularly so that you can break the negative ties with the people who have hurt you either personally or in business. By harbouring negative thoughts about them, you are hurting yourself more, not them. The thoughts are in your mind, not theirs, and they are your perception of what really is. And what really is may be something completely different.

Richard Branson believes you should always forgive the people you have fallen out with, no matter how difficult that might be. When he was in legal battle with British Airways, it was an extremely tough period in the life of Virgin Airlines and Branson could have lost his business. Within six months of the case being settled, Branson rang the chief executive of BA and invited him to lunch. Why? To clear the air (excuse the pun!). By doing so, Branson could move ahead with his business without having the negative energy surrounding his mind and the animosity that inevitably one would have in such situations.

By not having forgiveness, you are damaging yourself more than the other party. You are internalising your feelings and holding on to the negative thoughts. This will lead only to more negativity and illness. And if you bring all the other elements I speak about in this chapter together, you can see clearly how you can become caught up in a vicious circle. Free yourself of the negative energy and learn to "forgive others for what they have done, as they know not what they do".

ASK FOR HELP

A lot of people I come across have great difficulty in asking for help. I was one of these people. I wouldn't even ask for directions when I got lost. But through the years, I realised the quickest way to get somewhere is to ask for help. And people are only too willing to give help when asked. In everything that you do in life, somebody has already done what you want to do. So they've already made all the mistakes and probably gone the long way around things. So do you not think they have some advice to give you to enable you to shorten your journey?

But sometimes, it's not as simple as that. Asking for help is an admission that we don't have all the answers. But yet again, that's your perception as to how other people will view you. People love to help other people. It's human nature. You're giving them a gift by asking them for help, because in return they can give you something of themselves – their knowledge, they can serve you.

You can ask for the support you need from God, whether you ask through prayer, meditation or conversation – putting your thoughts and needs into a request notifies your subconscious, which is the link between your conscious mind and God.

Ask, and it will be given to you; seek, and you will find; knock, and it will be opened to you.
Matthew, 7:7

When I asked to be closer to God in my time of desperation, that's exactly what happened. Events started to happen and new people came into my life to help me fulfil this request, without me even asking them. My request was answered faster than I could realise. It just happened. In almost everything that I do, I ask for help from God. If I'm doing something new in my business, I will ask for the right people to be introduced to me to help me know what I need to do. And every time, exactly the right person gets introduced to me.

It's an awful lot quicker than trying to figure things out for yourself. God wants to help you. His love for you is boundless.

MAINTAIN POSITIVE THOUGHTS

Our thoughts create our actions, which create our results. Paying close attention to your thoughts and keeping them positive and optimistic opens up the energy that allows you to connect with your intuition and your subconscious mind. You can change your state of mind and your physical state, just by your thoughts.

If you started to think about an emotionally painful experience you had in the past, you would be able to recall that experience with clarity. And if you continued to contemplate that experience for a while, you would notice that your breathing would change. It would become shallow, your outlook on life would change, even your physical body would recoil. Then if you were to clear those thoughts from your mind and think of a wonderful experience you had with all the fun and laughter, the exhilaration and the belief you could accomplish anything, and stay with those thoughts for a while, you would begin to recognise that your breathing would become stronger, you would be standing more erect and your outlook in life would be powerful. All of this is achieved simply though your thoughts.

At times when you're not feeling the best and you feel everything is going wrong around you, at that very point, you have the choice to be happy or to be sad. It's easier to continue to be sad and wallow in self-pity. As human beings, we enjoy it in a weird way. When things are going poorly for us, we have the choice to remain feeling poorly or to be happy. It's that simple. The hardest part is recognising that you are heading to feelings of being sad and then snapping out of it.

Your state of mind can be as simple as deciding to be happy, powerful, and confident. You can change your state just by the thoughts you harbour in your mind.

BE WILLING TO LEARN FROM MISTAKES

We all make mistakes; it's how we handle them that can make the difference in whether we are successful. Don't let your failures discourage you from moving forward or stop you altogether. Find the lesson in the failure and move forward, always keeping your vision or your purpose in mind.

Anything that shows up in your life that, at first glance, is trying to put you off course may mean instead that you have a lesson to learn. When at first glance, everything appears to be falling apart, or things are going wrong, or not going as smoothly as you would like, step back and see whether there is a lesson to be learnt in what is happening at that moment. Look back at obstacles or seemingly 'your worst nightmares' that occurred previously in your life and look at them from a different perspective: if there was a deeper lesson to be learnt from that incident, what would it be for you?

There will always be a pattern to how you behaved in similar situations. Try as much as possible to see what that pattern is. Have you started something and not completed it? Where else have you started something and not completed it? Have you come away angry from a discussion but you didn't say how you felt? Where else do you move away from a discussion feeling angry but you also didn't say what you felt? What do you think the lesson is? Should you begin to say how you feel in discussions where you feel angry? Where else are you not standing up for yourself? How's that working for you? Start to see the patterns that show up in your life.

Monitor the seemingly disastrous situations you find yourself in, or the situations where there is a negative emotion inside of you, and find the lesson that you need to learn. Once you learn the lesson and correct it, you never have to face that lesson ever again.

TRY SOMETHING NEW

Be open to new ideas and do different things. There are always better and smarter ways to do things. No one person has all the answers. Be open to different ways of doing things and new information. By trying something new on a regular basis, you are developing your brain to seek out new opportunities and build new neural pathways.

Everything new is a new experience. Your soul craves new experiences. With these new experiences, you will begin to see new opportunities for your business, and to think laterally.

MAKE YOUR OWN LUCK

I never liked being referred to as being 'lucky'. The truth of the matter is somebody isn't born 'lucky'. You create your own luck. And the harder you work, the luckier you become!

As you move forward with focus, determination, and faith, the doors to opportunities will open, but first you will have to recognise the opportunity, and then take the steps to walk through those doors of possibility. Develop your intuition and connection with God and you will be guided exactly where you need to be.

CONTRIBUTE TO OTHERS

Everything is energy. When you take everything and break it down into its parts, you get molecules, and then atoms. Break it down even further and what you have is energy. Every object, every human being, everything is energy. Therefore, money is also energy. And, like an electrical circuit, in order for energy to work, there has to be a flow. If you create a blockage in an energy field, you create a dis-ease. Therefore, you need to allow the flow of money to circulate. If you block money within your business, you are blocking that flow. Not only are you preventing the flow to others, you are also preventing the flow of that energy to you.

As part of the wealth you create in your business, to allow the flow, give a portion of your wealth to the places where you get your spiritual nourishment from. This can be to your church, a charity where you see spiritual work being carried out for other human beings, or where you feel you have received spiritual nourishment yourself that has touched your soul.

SERVE OTHERS

You are here to use your gifts and your talents and to carry out the work you have been called to do. You are here to be of service and to serve. That is to say, as a business leader, you are here to do the best you can do, and to be the best you can be. It's not about personal recognition, money or power. It's about being of service to God and doing God's work. What is the work you are to do? Find your purpose, your vision, and what you are being called to do.

Your calling doesn't mean becoming a priest or a nun. As a business leader, you are being called to do the work you are capable of doing with the gifts and the talents you have to be part of the mosaic of life. You will only ever be called to do the work you are capable of. By doing the best you can do, you are delivering value to your customers.

Who are your customers? They are your family, your clients, your consumers, your employees, your stakeholders, your community, your board of directors, your peers ... Your purpose is to serve and help people to accomplish what they want to accomplish. Be of service to others and you will develop a business that all your customers will want to be associated with.

Always look to the future, observe what others are doing around you in your marketplace and see how could it be done differently, more easily and more beneficially to your customers. Always be of service to the customers you wish to engage. Make your clients a success, make your customers winners, and then you will have a business that is sustainable. When you do a good job, probably you will develop twice as much business as you expect. Indeed, if you succeed in delighting customers, there will not be enough hours in the day.

ACKNOWLEDGE THE CONTRIBUTION OF OTHERS

No one person can build a business, an enterprise, or a dynasty by themselves. Acknowledge people as they contribute to helping you achieve your goals, the people who enable you to do what you set out to do, or guide you on your path. Even if it's just a simple "Thank You". See the God in every person you encounter who has helped you be where you are.

KEEP AN OPTIMISTIC ATTITUDE

Use your faith to see the 'best' in every circumstance and to understand that there is a purpose in all things if you keep your focus on your vision and move forward. Always look on the bright side … life is much easier to live that way and people will want to be around you and help you achieve your goal.

SURROUND YOURSELF WITH POSITIVE PEOPLE

Be particular about the people that you let into your life – both business and personal – because the way they look at life and the attitudes that they have will have an effect on you. Optimistic people can uplift you and negative people can drag you down.

HAVE NO FEAR

If fear is present, connection to your Higher Source is almost impossible because fear is a negative emotion, which keeps you blocked from hearing or connecting with your intuitive self. You are asked only to trust and believe. If you trust and believe, then there is no place for fear. In God we trust!

Fear is preventing you from an experience. Your life is about having as many experiences as possible. Your focus should be on the experience, not on the fear itself. Fear is created in your head and, therefore, can be removed. When you get past fear, you have freedom. Where is fear holding you back in your business?

STOP WORRYING

Therefore I tell you, do not worry about your life, what you will eat or drink; or about your body, what you will wear. Is not life more than food, and the body more than clothes? Look at the birds of the air; they do not sow or reap or store away in barns, and yet your heavenly Father feeds them. Are you not much more valuable than they? Can any one of you by worrying add a single hour to your life? And why do you worry about clothes? See how the flowers of the field grow. They do not labour or spin. Yet I tell you that not even Solomon in all his splendour was dressed like one of these. If that is how God clothes the grass of the field, which is here today, and tomorrow is thrown into the fire, will he not much more clothe you—you of little faith? So do not worry, saying, 'What shall we eat?' or 'What shall we drink?' or 'What shall we wear?'. For the pagans run after all these things, and your heavenly Father knows that you need them. But seek first his kingdom and his righteousness, and all these things will be given to you as well. Therefore do not worry about tomorrow, for tomorrow will worry about itself. Each day has enough trouble of its own.
Matthew, 6:25-34

You will always be provided for. Worry is a useless emotion – a waste of energy. My brother used to say, as we were growing up, "99% of worry is unproductive" and he was right.

Trust and believe in what you are doing, focus on today not tomorrow. And don't be attached to material things. Yes, it is absolutely fine and right to have splendid luxuries and wealth, but not to be attached to them. Be indifferent, be free from them. If who you are is represented by what you have, the car that you drive or the house that you live in – is that really you? Yes, have those things and have more, but be who you truly are.

Give yourself the freedom of not being attached to the material things. If they were stripped away from you, what do you have left? You have yourself – just you. Find yourself first, go within and find who you truly are.

KNOW YOU ARE GOING TO SUCCEED

Having faith in yourself and a power much larger than yourself keeps the doors open to your energy source. Know that being connected, listening and doing what is necessary will lead you to success. The only thing you need to do is to follow your intuition and it will guide you in what you need to do in business.

No matter what decision I had to make in my career and business, despite the decisions seeming crazy to people on the outside, they always ended up being the right decisions. Successful business people know they are going to succeed. They have a feeling inside of them that they just know they are to be successful, that they have a right to be successful. They look at their business as a vocation. It's just about getting there and being successful. Do you have this same mindset?

You are more powerful beyond your wildest dreams. Your motivation determines your goals. You are what you want to be.

CONCLUSION

The business world is rapidly changing, and while businesses of today and tomorrow will use some of the time-tested successful methods from business of the past, they will be required to be constantly flexible in their ability to adjust and grow as new technologies and a new spirituality in the way that we relate to each other become stronger forces in business at all levels.

But one thing has not changed, and will never change, when it comes to creating a successful business, and that is that people with goals succeed because they know where they are going … you become what you think about. And business leaders of the future will not only have to be clearer on their goals, those goals will have to be tied into a vision, a passion and a purpose.

We can all make a change. Our inner want is to make a difference, be of value and of worth, but throughout our life we get battered and bruised. We get knocked down and, sometimes, it's hard to get back up again. We find ourselves lost and not knowing what we are supposed to be doing because it all seems too hard.

We often 'think' too much when in fact we need to be 'not thinking' and just be silent … looking inside ourselves for what we truly want. Yet when we get a glimpse of what could be possible, sometimes we can find ourselves coming up with all the reasons why we 'cannot'. In fact, some people get so overwhelmed with the whole process that they simply call it a 'mid-life crisis' and either give up or quit and go in a totally different direction. But that feeling of being overwhelmed is most likely just a case of something inside of you saying, "Wake up, please, I am here and now it's time to get on with some real work, God's work".

Simply put, ours is not to reason why or how, ours is to figure out the 'what' (our vision and purpose), and we only find that by going inside ourselves. When we find the 'what,' the how and why will look after themselves as our purpose and our vision become clearer. We just have to awaken the sleeping giant within us all. It all starts with our vision … our dream of what could be.

One thing sets the true entrepreneur apart from the rest of business leaders and that is that they have an unwavering sense of being successful. They just know they are going to be successful at whatever they put their mind to. They have no fear of failure and, despite what their peers might say to put them off, they continue to believe in themselves and strive for what they envision.

Entrepreneurs of tomorrow will have the task of building a financially successful venture, while at the same time being concerned with sustainability, accountability and ethical behaviour. For the business leaders of tomorrow, simplicity is the key: be real, be aware, be fair, be human, be authentic, be open, be ethical, be inclusive, be truthful and be responsible.

This book was written to guide you in creating your business and helping you integrate the best of the 'old' and the powerful thought processes that have existed for centuries with the technologies of today to create a successful business for the future.

At the start of this book, I asked you to open your mind to spirituality, the wisdom of gaining your own truth. It's my belief that the more you bring spirituality into business, the more successful you will be. I have seen it manifest through my own clients. I also believe that bringing spirituality into business will play a significant part of successful business for the future and, therefore, as business leaders, we all need to evolve.

Imagine an organisation where all people within it worked according to the principles outlined in this book – on spiritual principles, on community principles, on universal principles – where each and every one of your employees knew the true vision for the business, their values were aligned, and they harnessed the power of their own Higher Mind for the purpose of developing a business that was for the better of the wider community. What kind of a business would that be? What kind of a community would we then live in? How different would the world be?

As a human race, we're evolving at a rate of knots. We're making technology advances like never before. But some parts of us as a human race, in my belief, are not evolving. The way we make decisions has been the same for centuries. Decisions around conflict, war, the poor in society, the countless deaths everyday in famine-stricken countries, pandering to big industry at the forfeit of what is right for this planet as a whole. This is where we need to evolve.

There is only one thing we need to do throughout our life and that is love. When you look at the acronym I have used for this book, **EVOLVE**, there is no mistake as to why I have chosen this word. Yes, we need to evolve in everything that we do. But more importantly we have to love.

Take the first four letters from 'evolve' and spell them backwards, and you get LOVE. We have to love ourselves, our other human beings and we have to 'be' love. When you truly understand who you are, that God is within each and every one of us, and you can see the soul in everybody; you can only be love. In every decision that you make, in every action that you take, in every thought that you have, strive for love and then, as a human race, we might achieve something truly remarkable.

Yes, it's tough to do. Yes, it's hard to see the love in others when they have done something against us. Life can be hard, sometimes. But we have to start with ourselves. And every day, we have to start with the intention of being love. What better intention is there to start the day with? The ripple effect that you will have will go far beyond what you can imagine. In this way, we really are building businesses for the future that we can be proud of.

Purposely, the title of this book is **EVOLVE**. It is a command if you will, to evolve as a person and as a soul – to remember who you truly are and to take the lessons from this lifetime.

Throughout each of the aspects I have discussed in this book has been spirituality – your connection with God or whatever title you choose to use. When you bring all of these aspects together, you are truly successful. All I can ask of you is for you to gain your own wisdom and choose to know God for yourself. Although success is personal, and means different things for each individual, for me, success is knowing who you truly are, being your authentic self, and living your true purpose each and every day.

There are so many lessons in this book, and there are so many things I want you to gain from reading it. For that reason, I encourage you to read it several times. As you evolve, you will gain new meaning from this book each and every time you read it. Take the lessons in this book and incorporate them into your personal and business life. Put them into practice and become a business leader of the future.

It's part of my vision that this message will get to as many people around the world as possible. I ask you to share the message of this book. Make the people that you know aware that it exists so that they too can gain from its knowledge. Bit by bit, we can change this world and make it a better place for everybody.

We can do no great things, only small things with great love.
Mother Teresa

There is a source of power much greater than we can imagine within ourselves and successful people all over the world have understood this truth for centuries. Throughout this book, I have given you all the connections that I have made in order for you to make your own mind up. Once you do, then it's up to you to tap into this powerful source. I wish you every success in your life.

Let your light shine

Our deepest fear is not that we are inadequate.
Our deepest fear is that we are powerful beyond measure.
It's our light, not our darkness, that most frightens us.
We ask ourselves, 'Who am I to be brilliant, gorgeous, talented or
fabulous?'
Actually, who are you not to be?
You are a child of God.
Your playing small does not serve the world.
There is nothing enlightened about shrinking
so that other people won't feel insecure around you.
We are all meant to shine as children do.
We were born to make manifest the glory of God that is within us.
It's not just in some of us, it's in everyone.
As we let our own light shine,
we unconsciously give other people permission to do the same.
As we are liberated from our own fear,
our presence automatically liberates others.

Marianne Williamson

BOOKS AND
RESOURCES

BOOKS

Covey, Dr. Stephen R. (2004). *The 7 Habits of Highly Effective People*, New York: The Free Press (originally published 1990).

Dyer, Dr. Wayne (1989). *You'll See It When You Believe It*, New York: HarperCollins Publishers.

Haanel, Charles F. (1912). *The Master Key System*, Charles F. Haanel: Burnaby, BC, Canada: Ishtar Publishing.

Hay, Louise L. (1996). *Gratitude A Way of Life*, Carlsbad, CA: Hay House Inc.

Hill, Napoleon (2008). *Think & Grow Rich*, Seattle, WA: CreateSpace (originally published 1937).

Jones, Laurie Beth (1995). *Jesus, CEO*, New York: Hyperion Books.

Murphy, Joseph (1988). *The Power of Your Subconscious Mind*, Upper Saddle River, NJ: Prentice Hall.

Orwell, George (1964). *Animal Farm*, Harmondsworth, Middx: Penguin Books.

Ray, Michael (1996). *The New Entrepreneurs,* San Francisco, CA: New Leaders Press.

Ruiz, Don Miguel (1997). The Four Agreements, San Rafael, CA: Amber-Allen Publishing Inc.

Saint Teresa of Avila (2010). *Autobiography*, Mineola, NY: Dover Publications.

Seligman, Dr. Martin E.P. (2002). *Authentic Happiness*, New York: The Free Press.

Williamson, Marianne (1996). *A Return to Love: Reflections on the Principles of a Course in Miracles*, New York: Harper Collins.

RESOURCES & WEBSITES

Signature Strengths Exercise - **www.authentichappiness.org**
Determining Your Values Exercise – **www.thebookevolve.com**

ABOUT THE
AUTHOR

Paul Davis FCMA CMC is a leading business growth specialist in Ireland and has turned every loss-making business he has worked with into profit. He is known for being a classic lateral thinker, for his strong commercial acumen, and his exceptional ability to identify the constraints of a business and, with his down-to-earth approach, quickly implement plans for change.

Having trained as a Management Accountant and become a Certified Management Consultant, Paul worked across a wide-range of industry sectors, including: consultancy, construction, high- and low-tech manufacturing, service, and nationwide retail.

To date, Paul has supported countless organisations and transformed several unprofitable enterprises into multi-million euro successes. Along with running his own successful business, Paul has delivered many thought-provoking and practical business growth workshops, and has had articles published in national newspapers and business magazines.

You can find out more about Paul and how he works with clients by visiting **www.davisbusinessconsultants.com.**

You can contact Paul with your comments and feedback:

Mail: Minley House, Newtownpark Avenue, Blackrock, Co Dublin, Ireland

Email: evolve@davisbusinessconsultants.com

Website: www.davisbusinessconsultants.com

LinkedIn: www.linkedin.com/in/pauldavisdublin

Twitter: www.twitter.com/pauldavisdublin

Facebook: www.facebook.com/davisbusinessconsultants

And for more commentary and information, visit **www.thebookevolve.com**.

OAK TREE PRESS

Oak Tree Press develops and delivers information, advice and resources for entrepreneurs and managers. It is Ireland's leading business book publisher, with an unrivalled reputation for quality titles across business, management, HR, law, marketing and enterprise topics. NuBooks is its recently-launched imprint, publishing short, focused ebooks for busy entrepreneurs and managers.

In addition, through its founder and managing director, Brian O'Kane, Oak Tree Press occupies a unique position in start-up and small business support in Ireland through its standard-setting titles, as well training courses, mentoring and advisory services.

Oak Tree Press is comfortable across a range of communication media – print, web and training, focusing always on the effective communication of business information.

Oak Tree Press, 19 Rutland Street, Cork, Ireland.

T: + 353 21 4313855 F: + 353 21 4313496.

E: info@oaktreepress.com W: www.oaktreepress.com.